PROLOGUE:

A Prelude to My Bullshit

There are two types of people: those who play Cards Against Humanity, and those who don't.

For the uninitiated, Cards Against Humanity is an adult card game in which the outcome depends solely on one person's opinion of the other players' cards. The rules are simple: each player draws ten white cards, or answer cards. These spout witty phrases or name specific things, like "The entire internet" or "Donald Trump". At the beginning of each round, one player is designated as the judge. That player grabs a black card, or a question card, that sets up the round. Once the judge reads this card, the other players take turns playing whichever one of their white cards best fits the description on the judge's black card.

There are different reasons a judge will choose a given answer. Some play the game straight, laying the card that makes the most sense. Stupid people, which I have dealt with on many occasions, will pick the cards with the least number of words. And then there are people like me, who pick the cards that make them laugh the hardest.

The key to winning is understanding what kinds of answers your judge prefers. When it comes to humor, that can be a delicate balancing act. Even people with a sense of humor might stray from the more off-putting outcomes.

I buy into the game's marketing slogan: it's a party game for horrible people.

There are certain combinations of words that cause someone to laugh. Have you ever been at a funeral, or a wedding rehearsal, or a synagogue, and you find yourself laughing at the most inappropriate time? A joke you heard last week pops in your head, and for a few seconds you're the center of attention?

Here's an example of a typical round, the way I play it. The judge will play a black card that says, "I can't wait to go to _____ because it's the funnest place on Earth!" More than likely, I've been sitting with a deck of unplayable cards the whole game. Half of my deck includes the names of celebrities or political figures, which I can't figure into any kind of joke whatsoever. But there is one card that I've been holding onto this whole time, one that I'm dying to play if I can just get the judge to put down the right card. And I finally get my opportunity.

Going back to what I said earlier, it pays to know how the judge makes his selection. The answer card I have in question, while only one word, can be hard to pronounce for someone with a third-grade reading level. Playing the card with Karen as the judge isn't the wisest choice.

My best friend Matt, despite his warped sense of humor, typically plays the game straight. He would be looking for an answer like "Disneyland" or "Hawaii", so playing my card with him as the judge wouldn't be a good use of my answer.

Then there's my little brother, Glenn, who understands my sense of humor and shares my sensibilities. And luckily for me, he's the judge this round.

The rest of the players have already submitted their white answer cards to Glenn. Everyone is waiting for me to put down my answer. With my card face-down, I slide my answer to

Glenn's pile of white cards.

Glenn turns over the four answer cards. He begins to read them out loud. "The five-hour drive to Vegas," he says indifferently. "Okay." He moves on to the next one. "My stupid fucking son." I let out a bit of a snicker. I can't help it. It's a funny answer, even if it doesn't fit Glenn's description. Glenn then breaks out in uncontrollable laughter. Deep down, I start to get a little nervous. If Glenn is laughing this hard, then he probably already picked the best answer. He moves on to the third card. "A mime having a stroke." He looks around the table questioningly. "I'm not sure how that translates to the funnest place on Earth." His eyes then go to the fourth card. My card. The one card that could send me on a one-way ticket straight to Hell. But if I made the right choice, it's also the card that could win me the game.

Glenn examines the card. He looks down at his original black card. He quietly reads the black card out loud again, just to affirm that what he sees in his hand is real. "'I can't wait to go to _____ because it's the funnest place on Earth'." He looks directly at me, to which I give my usual response whenever someone gets one of my answer cards: "Don't look at me. I just play the cards. I don't write them."

"Seriously, bro?" Glenn asks. He covers his eyes with the brim of his hand. Then he starts laughing harder than I've ever seen him laugh. He gets so hysterical that everyone else at the table can't help but laugh, too. And they don't even know which card I played.

Glenn puts my white card face up so that everyone can see. The card I played was Auschwitz.

Matt shakes his head, but I know deep down, he's trying really hard not to laugh. "Lenny! That's terrible!"

Karen's boyfriend Bill also shakes his head, but even he can't stop laughing. It's not because he thinks my response is funny. He gets my sense of humor. In fact, everyone around the table gets my sense of humor. They might not understand it, but they expect those kinds of answers from me.

When I play, I play to win.

If you're overly sensitive, or you have a thin skin, or you're conservative, and you don't think jokes about the Holocaust are funny, then you've probably already closed the book, made some kind of grunting sound, and are on your way back to the bookstore for a refund. That's fine by me: I still get my royalty check. And there's a good chance I'm not writing this for you, anyways.

For those who would like to keep reading: thank you.

Hopefully the title of this book is an indication of things to come. But truthfully, my intention isn't to offend or stir up trouble. It's to clarify my stand on things, namely who I am versus who others perceive me to be. And there are a number of different perceptions, based on the heated comments I get on my Facebook posts.

Back to my game-winning Cards Against Humanity response.

First of all, I am Jewish. I went to Sunday school, I studied the atrocities of the Holocaust in great detail, and I've seen *Schindler's List* dozens of times. I know there's nothing funny about six million people being sent to their deaths. And I don't pretend that making jokes about the Holocaust isn't in poor taste – it is.

The reason I thought my card was funny was that it was unexpected. Remember that whole paragraph where I talked about laughing at inappropriate times? I was betting on the idea that playing "Auschwitz" would get a laugh because first, it's an offensive answer. It's also the one that no one expected.

Would it have been funny to my parents? Or to my conservative aunts and uncles? How about my cousins, who gang up on me the minute I say something they don't like? Probably not. But then again, why the hell are a bunch of prudes playing Cards

Against Humanity?

In high school, I played the "How offensive can I get?" game all the time. The words "inappropriate" were uttered to me more times than I can count. But the more I thought about it, the more I realized that "inappropriate" was a relative term. The same thing that offends one person will also make someone else's day. Do you think most stand-up comedians worry about what jokes offend certain people? That's why the best comedians usually end up offending *everyone*. They also know that along the way, they're going to make someone laugh. The rewards outweigh the risk. It's okay to offend one specific group of people.

Just as long as thirty other groups find it funny.

I know there are plenty of people who think that offending people is insensitive and wrong. There's nothing wrong with those people. I think it's great that there are people out there who defend minorities, and remind people like me that making fun of a certain situation, or certain people, is unacceptable.

I just choose not to associate with those people.

Those people are perfectly nice, but there's no way in hell I would know how to gel with someone like that. I say what's on my mind, and I don't go around wondering what would offend who. That would drive me fucking nuts.

So, occasionally I say offensive things. And while I might upset a small group of people along the way, a lot of the times, for better or for worse, it starts some really engaging conversations. And more importantly, it gets someone to laugh. I wish I could say things without the internet beating the shit out of me. But that's why the internet was invented: so we could make people feel like dirt from the comforts of our living rooms. No need to literally burn someone at the stake when we can do it figuratively from behind our computer screens, right?

In my defense, I'm a pretty good guy on most days. But I

feel like sometimes I'm expected to play a certain role, and at times that role is the *bad* guy. If I was a Disney character, I'd be Wreck-It Ralph. I'm the one desperately trying to prove that I'm a good guy. I'm the one who wants the shiny metal, even though life's programming constantly keeps telling me: I'm the villain.

If that's too metaphorical for you, then let me say this: I don't try to offend anyone. But I'm also not going to apologize when I do. And it cuts deep whenever I'm publicly crucified for putting an idea out there that you disagree with. If you disagree with me, that's fine. Reading this, you might come to realize that a lot of my ideas are unpopular, anyways. Some people have actually questioned my sanity, not understanding that I just walk to the beat of a different drum. And no matter how offensive I get, let's not pretend that there aren't people out there, major media moguls, who have said and done far worse. All you have to do is look at our former president to understand the validity of that point.

And if you've read all of this and you still come to the conclusion that I'm just an insensitive, immoral pig who possesses the charm of a hairless goat, then all I can say to that is:

Please, with all sincerity, go fuck yourself.

CHAPTER 1:

My 8-Bits on Movies, Retro Video Games, and Creative Writing

I was five-years-old when I first saw Star Wars.

I sat in Janice Lovejoy's den, in front of a 27" wood-paneled television, cross-legged and experiencing what would become one of the most inspiring movies in my life.

I saw images from the film before, in segments from *The Muppet Babies*, and in storybooks – the ones that came with .45 records, where a narrator read the story and played a chime when it was time to turn the page. I vaguely remember getting a birthday cake molded in the shape of R2-D2 for my second birthday, before I had any idea who he was.

Even in 1988, the impact of the *Star Wars* trilogy was well engraved in American culture. Much like the classic Universal monsters, you didn't have to experience the films to know the iconic imagery. But it was something else entirely if you *had* seen them. It was like hearing about all the attractions at Disney World, and finally getting to experience the rides.

That opening shot following the crawl, with that gigantic Star Destroyer drifting overhead as it pursued Princess Leia in her Tantive IV – back then, I didn't know it had a name – was so impressive. My eyes were transfixed to the screen, the images dancing across my eyeballs, as the Rebels prepared to be boarded by an evil force I had yet to witness. Those white doors blasted open, and a horde of white-clad Stormtroopers entered the ship's corridor, blasting everything in sight. Bodies fell left and right, as two recognizable droids tried to make it through the death and rubble surrounding them. When the smoke cleared, the sterile white environment gave way to one of the most awe-inspiring character entrances in movie history: the introduction of Darth Vader. He stood at two meters tall, his hands coolly at his hips as he surveyed the damage. His raspy breathing filled the room, the lights on his front armor blinking on and off. To a five-year-old kid, it was a lot to process.

I didn't know I was watching a movie that would forever change cinematic history. I wasn't aware of its cultural impact, that it had such a widespread fanbase, and that during its initial premiere in the summer of '77, millions of people lined up for blocks, many of them decked out in full costume, waiting to get their first glimpse of George Lucas's expansive universe. All I knew was that I was watching something special, something that no other movie could emulate.

In the 80's, there weren't a lot of behind-the-scenes documentaries. This was before the advent of DVD, where special features, deleted scenes and Director's Cuts didn't exist.

I didn't understand that movies were *crafted*, that there were hundreds of people pulling the strings, shedding blood and tears to get these things made. I didn't realize that all this stuff had to be photographed, edited, and mixed down to create a final product. At five-years-old, it never occurred to me that people could earn a living making movies.

It amazes me how frequently the world of *Star Wars* would weave in and out of my life. It refused to go away, like most of those 80's franchises trying to make a comeback now. But *Star Wars* always had a way of finding me. Long after my love for *Teenage Mutant Ninja Turtles* and *Power Rangers* was phased out, *Star Wars* always came back, and I answered the call. There's a reason why so many people are enamored with this franchise. Film scholars, and even the cast and crew, have tried to sum it up in so many words. It's impossible.

Movies have always been a constant in my life. I'm always looking to expand my knowledge of film, even if I don't get to watch as much as I'd like. I spend my days off on Amazon, or carousing the movie section at Best Buy, trying to find titles that will make a worthy addition to my growing collection. I have an insatiable appetite for cinema, and I spend most of my increasingly limited free time watching something.

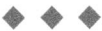

Around the time I was introduced to Luke Skywalker's heroic journey, I discovered the other great love in my life.

Once again, I was at Janice Lovejoy's house. While my parents worked, I spent most afternoons penned up in Janice's den, where she subjected me to a lot of cheesy 80's cartoons and Disney movies. This probably explains my later fixation toward graphic horror films.

One morning, I came over and saw Janice's six-year-old son, Mark, locked in front of his TV. In his hands was some sort of rectangular control pad. I had never seen anything like it. There was a cross-looking directional pad and two red buttons, marked *B* and *A*. As Mark watched the images on the screen, he was simultaneously pushing the buttons on the controller, as if he were controlling the images.

The character on the screen was a heavyset man with a moustache, a hat, and red suspenders. And he was running. And jumping. He did that a lot. The object of this little fiasco, I guessed, was to jump on these little red, squishy monsters with beaks and no torsos. They were basically heads with feet. There were also enemy turtles. Something else strange that happened – when this pixelated man jumped beneath a shiny gold brick, he would activate a coin block, or sometimes, unleash a mushroom that would make him *bigger*. And when this man finally got to his destination, he jumped on top of a flagpole and proceeded to enter a castle. This would take him to another location, where he continued to fight these weird monsters.

I was mesmerized. Words couldn't express what I was feeling. Mark was controlling the TV.

"What is this?" I asked, taking a seat on the carpeting next to him. We were two little kids transfixed to the TV screen, the light bouncing off our brainwashed faces.

"Super Mario Bros.," Mark said, completely expressionless.

Even though I wasn't actually playing, it felt like I was. I was totally immersed in this new experience. It wasn't just what I was seeing, but those sound effects: the *ba-ding!* of collecting coins, the *ba-doop!* whenever Mario jumped on an enemy, the *blarp-blarp-blarp* when he explored a pipe. And that memorable music. On rare occasions, there were even fireworks at the end of a level. It was intoxicating.

"Let me try," I said, and I reached over for the controller.

"Heck, no!" Mark said, and leaned away from me so I couldn't reach it. "You're not allowed to play." I had just experienced a five-year-old's equivalent to blue balls.

My heart sank. Something else I should mention: I was an extremely passive kid. I didn't know how to argue or fight. I was still an only child, and I didn't interact that much with other kids. Janice had a hair-trigger temper and didn't put up with any kiddy shit, as I saw whenever Mark and his older bully of a sister, Maddison, fought.

All I could do was sit there, watching Mark hog up the screen, and praying that he would leave at some point so I could get a turn.

From down the hall, I heard Janice scream from her bedroom: "Mark Anthony Lovejoy, march your little butt into that kitchen and eat breakfast before the bus gets here. What did I tell you about playing that game right before school?"

With the push of a button, Mark paused the screen. He got up and ran into the kitchen. Now was my chance.

I picked up the controller, still warm from Mark's grimy little hands. I pushed every button, trying to figure out how to un-pause the game. Finally, the music kicked back on. I tapped the directional pad, and Mario took a few steps. When I kept my thumb pressed on the button, Mario started walking. Within seconds, I encountered my first enemy. I panicked. I scrambled to push all the buttons, desperately trying to figure out which one of them made Mario jump.

It was too late. The little red beaky thing with no torso (called a goomba) touched Mario, and before I knew what happened, Mario was spazzing out. He made this weird little sound, then disappeared off the screen with a "blip." Then there was this little musical piece, as if the game was saying, "Nah-nah-na-nah-nah!" But before I knew it, the game started right back up, and once again, there was Mario, standing at the beginning of this strange little world, ready to take on more monsters. It was then I realized: Mario had *lives*. He could die more than once.

I gave it another try. I soon realized that the A button made him jump, so I finally overcame a few enemies. Within seconds, I was fully addicted, immersed in the game. There was no stopping me.

I heard a pair of stomping feet behind me. "I told you, you can't play!" Mark screamed. He grabbed the controller from my hand, pausing the game. "Did you make me lose a life?"

I slowly nodded my head, like a puppy who knows it just shit on the rug.

Mark reached over and unplugged the controller from

a grey plastic box. "You're not allowed to play," he said, and marched off down the hall.

Imagine being addicted to one of the strongest drugs in the world, getting a small taste, and then having it snatched away just before you get high.

Before I knew what happened, Janice stormed down the hall. She grabbed the controller from Mark's hand, bent down, and with one cupped hand squeezed his cheeks together, bringing his face mere inches from hers.

"Why are you being such a mean little snot this morning?" she hissed through grit teeth.

With his cheeks still clenched in the palm of her hand, Mark struggled to get the words out. "Mmmm, he dsn't knew hew to play," he managed.

"Stop being so bossy and get your ass ready for school."

Mark ran down the hall without another word.

Truth be told, I was always afraid of Janice. She was a big woman, for one thing. But she moved fast, and she spoke with the venom of a cobra. When she talked to you, she made direct eye contact, like she was out to win the world championship of a staring contest. It didn't matter if you were a guest in her house: if you stepped out of line, she treated you like you were one of her own kids.

As she approached me with the controller, I thought she was going to shoo me into the den and force me to watch *Pete's Dragon*. To my utter bewilderment, she handed me the controller. "Here you go, sweetie. You have a turn."

Very seldom had I grinned so much.

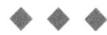

I played all day long, not even taking a break to eat lunch. I couldn't get that far, but I just couldn't get tired of breaking bricks, shooting fireballs, and giving that nasty dragon creature (who I later learned was named King Koopa) another go before plunging back into the lava in level 1-4.

By the time my dad picked me up around 3:30-ish, I was the full-on equivalent of a heroin junkie. I was addicted to Nintendo, and there was no 12-step program for what I had.

I was mildly aware that I also had to pee – badly. But I knew that at any minute, Mark and his sadistic sister would march through that door, and then my game time would be all but over.

"Come on, son," my dad said, in a hurry to leave.

I sat on my knees, doing the piss dance – that's when you shimmy from side-to-side when your bladder is screaming at you to find the nearest toilet.

But as soon as my dad saw what I was playing, even he was impressed. "What's this?"

"Your boy hasn't taken his eyes off that screen since Sandy dropped him off this morning," Janice said. "He's hooked. You might want to put him through some kind of detox program."

"What is it?" my dad asked again.

"Super Mario Bros., for Nintendo," Janice replied. "Got it for the kids for Christmas. Since then, their Atari's just been gathering dust in the basement."

My dad looked at me. There I was, violently shifting in place, trying to keep from pissing myself, as I once again guided Mario through King Koopa's ravenous 8-bit dungeon.

He stroked his chin. "Nintendo, huh? I'll have to look into that." As I continued dancing in place on the floor, Janice's eyes widened with panic. She realized why I was dancing like that.

"Lenny, you'd better go to the bathroom. I just had this carpeting installed."

It didn't matter, anyway – another one of Koopa's fireballs killed me, sending me directly to Game Over Land. I shot up from my place on the floor, doing a beeline for the bathroom. I didn't even bother closing the door. I had no idea until that moment just how badly I had to piss.

◆ ◆ ◆

Without even asking for it, about a month later, right before the start of summer, I had my very own Nintendo Entertainment System. One of my dad's friends had just bought something called a Sega Genesis and was getting rid of his old library of games. It was just my luck.

Today, it's common to find digital copies of just about any video game you'd want to play. But if you head over to Amazon or eBay to price a physical copy, the cost on some of them is out of this world.

It's weird to think how much a lot of those old games are valued at, when you consider that old VHS tapes – hell, even DVDs – can be found for pennies on the dollar.

Nintendo cartridges typically came in big grey boxes, roughly the size of VHS tapes, and came packaged with a full-color instruction manual. Usually, we threw out the grey box and did our best to save the instruction manual, even though most of the games were self-explanatory.

I had a pretty good collection, too: the popular *Super Mario Bros./Duck Hunt* combo cart; *Castlevania* and its sequel, *Castlevania II: Simon's Quest*; *Kid Icarus*, which I never really figured out; *Contra*, which my older cousin and I would always play when he came over to babysit me on the home front; and while it would be a couple of years before I owned the original *Legend of Zelda*, I did own a copy of *Zelda II: The Adventure of Link*.

Some of you may be screaming blasphemy, but this was not a world where *Zelda* was this immensely popular IP with dozens of titles to its name. The original game was this kind of overnight sleeper hit, and in the late 80's, right as I got my Nintendo, *Zelda II* was the newer game. While today, *Zelda II* is considered the red-headed stepchild of the franchise, back then, there were actually people who favored that second game over the original.

For those not initiated, *Legend of Zelda* was a milestone because it was one of the first games that allowed players to explore. You didn't have to complete a set of stages in a pre-determined order, like in *Super Mario Bros*. Instead, you controlled the game from an overhead perspective, and you could go in any direction the game allowed you to. Some areas were tougher than others, prompting the player to find power-ups and weapon upgrades earlier in the game. But as far as what order you played the game in, that was left up to you. There were a lot of puzzles to solve, many of them having no obvious solutions; and a lot of the items were hidden so well that you either had to read *Nintendo Power*, a gaming magazine that offered all kinds of gaming tips, or listen in to conversations your friends had at school.

Zelda II took a different approach. First of all, it had more in common with an RPG, like *Final Fantasy*, than it did with the original *Zelda*. Part of the game was played from an overhead perspective, but when you battled enemies, the game switched to a side-scrolling view, which was more typical of the games from that era. While there were dozens of magic items to find, the majority of the gameplay focused on level grinding: a term common in RPGs, in which the player finds an area to sit around in and gain experience in order to level up their character. My dad's friend, Don, who bought the Genesis, was a big fan of this type of gameplay, and actually shit on the original game because of its cryptic elements.

Throughout that summer, my parents had many arguments about my constant need to shut myself in my room and play Nintendo all day. I'll admit, sitting on your ass and playing video games isn't a healthy pastime, but I was never into athletics or sports. I was fine with sitting on my ass all summer.

My mom argued that I needed to go outside, smell the fresh air, and play with friends. I wasn't allowed to step three feet out of her sight, but yeah, go outside and play with friends.

My dad's argument was that video games were helping my hand-eye coordination, and he used *Zelda* as a prime example. Whenever he argued this to my mom, he would say: "With *Zelda,* Lenny has to actually draw himself a map of where he's been, what objects he found, and where to go next. I'll be damn skippy if playing baseball is going to teach him the same thing."

To this day, my dad will use that exact same argument. My dad never even picked up a Nintendo controller, but he swears up and down that video games enhance hand-eye coordination.

But it wasn't long before even my dad got tired of my constant sitting around. I was a pretty lazy kid. As soon as I got home from school, before I did any homework, I was off playing *Castlevania*, whipping zombies and vampire bats as the heroic Simon Belmont. My dad put a stop to that right away.

"You bring home anything less than a solid B on your report card, I'm going to unplug your Nintendo and have myself a little barbeque in the backyard. It'll be ten years before you even see another video game in this house, so you'd better start cracking open those books."

This was also when my parents started pushing me to find more physical outdoor activities. I played Tee Ball for a couple of seasons, but since I didn't really want to be there, I wasn't very good at it. I seemed to always sit in the outfield, and it's hard to concentrate when your dad's yelling from the bleachers, "You'd better be paying attention out there, or else no video games for a month!" Believe me, that didn't do anything to bolster my confidence. All it did was give the other players a laugh to see one of their teammates running to the dugout, crying because his dad was threatening to ground him in front of the entire team.

◆ ◆ ◆

I also joined the Cub Scouts. Janice Lovejoy was a den leader, and Mark was in the same troop. Cub Scouts grew on me, because I was with a group of boys who had most of the same interests. Even though I always had an urge to go home and put down some Nintendo time, and I didn't have a practical bone in my body, I admit, I enjoyed trying to build cars, whittling, and camping outdoors.

One night, Mark invited all of the scouts over for his birthday party. We were all around eight years old. Mark's oldest sister, Allison, rented *Friday the 13th Part 2*. I couldn't believe it. She rented an R-rated movie for a bunch of eight-year-olds! I was certain that at any minute, Janice Lovejoy would march through those drapes separating the den from the rest of the house, snatch out the tape and force us to watch *Mary Poppins*.

But I guess on this night she figured: boys will be boys.

Friday the 13th Part 2 was released in 1981, distributed by Paramount Pictures and directed by Steve Miner, who would later go on to direct *Friday the 13th Part III, House, Forever Young,* and *Halloween H2O*. I didn't know it at the time, because I didn't see any of the other movies, but this was the first film where Jason was the killer. I knew who Jason was. I had the Nintendo game, the one where Jason was dressed in purple spandex. Every kid at school knew who Freddy and Jason were, but very few saw the actual movies because obviously, we were all too young.

I also didn't expect Jason to be running around wearing a potato sack on his head. Where was the infamous hockey mask? I had no idea just how much the series evolved over the course of eight films.

There's one moment in particular that stands out to me, a defining moment for my childhood that would carry over into my awkward prepubescent years. In the film, actress Kirsten Baker, who portrays up-and-coming camp counselor Terry, goes for a little late-night skinny dipping. Little does she know that fellow camp counselor and perv, Scott, played by Russell Todd, is peaking in on her from the shore. There's a brief moment where Terry surfaces, fully nude, from the lake. It's an extreme wide shot, and if you blink, you'll miss it, but all the boys hooted and screamed when that scene came on. It was the first time I ever saw full-frontal nudity.

Naturally, the oldest kid rewound the tape over and over again. It was the eight-year-old equivalent of a bunch of drunks at a strip club surrounding an exotic dancer.

The other scene of note, and the one that ended up getting the movie shut off on us, was the chase sequence at the end. The attractive female lead Ginny, played by Amy Steel, was being pursued by Jason, who in this film was played by two actors: Warrington Gillette and Steve Dash. In the final moments, Ginny gets holed up in Jason's dilapidated shack, when she realizes that he's been keeping all of his victims, as well as his mother's severed head, as keepsakes. In order to confuse Jason, Ginny puts on Mrs. Voorhees' sweater and pretends to be his long-dead mother. At this point, the movie was deemed too scary for us, and Allison, who rented the movie in the first place, turned it off. It would be some time before I saw the rest of the flick.

◆ ◆ ◆

Like *Star Wars*, *Friday the 13th* left a lasting impression on me – that, and the experience of being with a bunch of horny, like-minded teenagers reacting to the movie. It was one of those rare bonding experiences you cherish for the rest of your life.

After that, I developed an unhealthy obsession with slasher movies.

One of the fondest memories I have as a kid was catching one of those films on television, usually in marathons, on a Friday the 13th or Halloween. USA and TNT were the two prime networks that aired them, but it was a bummer because they censored the nudity and cut back on the violence. It was never clear exactly what they edited out, because sometimes they showed what was close to the full scene, and other times, the scene was butchered.

At that age, seeing any graphic violence was a big deal. Most kids weren't allowed. That's why Barney was invented. I didn't realize that a lot of those movies, *Friday the 13th* in particular, underwent public scrutiny from parents, critics, and outraged religious groups.

The movies would also occasionally show up on HBO, but how I really got caught up in the series was when my dad took me to Blockbuster and rented them all.

This was another subject my parents disagreed on. My dad found it perfectly acceptable for his eight-year-old son to watch these R-rated gore fests. Before you make any kind of judgment on my dad's lax parenting skills, here's his reasoning.

According to my dad – and I back up his logic – if kids want to experience something, they're going to find a way to experience it, whether you like it or not. And the more you try to suppress it, the more curious they're going to get. It's why some pent-up nuns become full-fledged porn stars, and why some Orthodox Jewish girls eventually grow up having sexual fantasies about Santa Claus in the hot tub.

Or is that just me?

Like my growing Nintendo addiction, slasher movies – mainly the *Friday the 13th* and *Nightmare on Elm Street* films – became engraved in my weekly to-do lists. Every weekend, I stayed up into the early hours of the morning, trying to see how many of these movies I could cram into one long marathon session. I memorized the names of all the victims, and could tell you at the snap of a finger how they died and what weapons were used to dispatch them.

One time, in scouts, a den leader heard me talking about these films with the other boys. "I don't understand what's so great about those movies," he said as he passed us by. "They're all the same thing. Just different ways of killing people."

Even in my thirties, I still watch these films, mostly for the nostalgia factor. Looking back at what that den leader said, yeah, he was right. It's hard to argue that point. But at age nine, I didn't have a huge palette to draw from.

A lot of kids from my generation grew up absorbing movies. They watched *Godzilla* films, or the classic Universal monster movies, or they'd catch whatever B-movies were airing on USA's *Up All Night* or TNT's *Monster Vision*. I had a pre-ordained batch of movies I turned to for comfort food, and it stifled my awareness of other films I was missing out on. Think about the movies you watched in the 80's – *Lethal Weapon, Die Hard, RoboCop, Rambo, Rocky*. I missed out on a lot of those because I was obsessed with Freddy and Jason. At that point, *Star Wars* had been driven from my conscience. I was a kid entering the adult world because I saw some movies with blood and tits in them.

Throughout my pre-teen years, my uncle, who shared a lot of the same tastes in movies as me, took me to plenty of R-rated films in theaters. *Army of Darkness* was my introduction to the *Evil Dead* series, even though at the time, I just thought it was this goofy one-off movie. If only Sam Raimi was allowed to call it by its original title, *The Medieval Dead*, it would have been a little clearer. My uncle racked his brains for days trying to remember what the first two films were called, so we could rent them and see where the series began.

Alien 3, Jason Goes to Hell, Wes Craven's New Nightmare – they were all movies I saw in theaters when I was probably just a little too young to know any better.

Then he introduced me to a little film called *The Toxic Avenger*.

Toxic Avenger was one of those movies I always saw on store shelves but was afraid to rent it. There was a cartoon called *Toxic Crusaders*, a kind of *Ninja Turtles/Captain Planet* knock-off. In 1990, New Line Cinema released the first *Teenage Mutant Ninja Turtles* feature film. It was a big deal, because it was one of the first live-action adaptations of an animated series. In the 80's, if a cartoon was turned into a theatrical film, the studio upped the animation budget and stretched out the run time. Doing a live-action version of a cartoon, while more common today, was a revolutionary thing back then. Naturally, when I saw *Toxic Avenger* sitting on store shelves, I thought it was just another attempt at turning a cartoon series into a live-action movie.

Couldn't be further from the truth.

The Toxic Avenger was an independent film directed by Lloyd Kaufman and his partner, Michael Herz. Kaufman and Herz founded an independent film company, Troma, and were struggling to hit the big time with raunchy sex comedies like *The First Turn-On!* and *Squeeze Play!*

They decided to change it up with a superhero/slasher/romantic comedy that sort of transformed Troma into a pseudo-household name. To this day, Troma still makes and distributes

B-movies, and if you're unfamiliar with them, let's just say that there's nothing else quite like them. If you're like me, and you're tired of Hollywood constantly going back to the well with their unending barrage of reboots and remakes, then you should really check out Troma's catalogue. They don't exactly make top-tier entertainment. But *The Toxic Avenger* is their claim to fame, and it became one of my favorite movies of all time.

The Toxic Avenger follows this nerdy, borderline-retarded health spa janitor, Melvin, who falls victim to a harmful prank that results in him being submerged in a vat of toxic waste. He transforms into a mutant monster that resembles Swamp Thing mixed with the Jolly Green Giant, and goes around killing all the bad guys in Tromaville.

He's a monster superhero who *murders* bad guys.

There was nothing else like it. I was just getting into comic books, thanks to the recent *Death of Superman* craze, and as I just explained, I was a slasher movie addict. Putting those two things together in a low-budget film that featured lots of gore, sex, and overacting at its finest resulted in one of the most outlandish and entertaining movie experiences I'd ever been privy to. Every time I show the film to a different group of people, they go bananas, because it's unlike any movie they've ever seen. It's a great party film.

It even goes great with a bris.

Being raised Jewish meant that my two younger brothers and I had what's called a *bris*. It's a big Jewish celebration held one week after a baby is born, where family members come over and celebrate the baby's circumcision. I don't want to get into details – just Google "bris" and "circumcision" and you'll be all set.

In December of 1993, my parents brought home my baby brother, Glenn. I wanted no part of this whole *bris* thing, so naturally I stayed in my room. Fortunately, my parents invited some of the scouts to keep me company, so we spent the afternoon drowning out my new brother's screams by playing rounds of *Super Mario Kart* and watching *The Toxic Avenger*. It was one of the most memorable afternoons of my life.

◆ ◆ ◆

In the fourth grade, I was introduced to fiction writing. I spent the majority of my time watching movies, playing video games, reading comic books and indulging in the occasional R.L. Stine novel. I had a pretty intense imagination.

The teacher divided our class into groups of four or five students, and our job was to collectively come up with a fictional story and present it to the class. Each member was responsible for coming up with a different part of the story.

My group was largely uncreative. When it was our turn to present to the class, the other kids talked about how they got up in the morning, took a bath, brushed their teeth, took the bus to school – they were giving these little "slice of life" moments that make for terrible storytelling. These kids would have made awful screenwriters, because any screenwriter knows, nothing will cause a judge, a producer, or a director to roll their eyes faster than a bunch of scenes where nothing happens.

When it came time to tell my part of the story, I told how, as I was walking home from school, I realized I had a hole in one of my pant pockets, causing all of my loose change to roll around on the sidewalk. I started giving chase to a quarter, when I accidentally stomped on it with my foot. The quarter flattened, turned into a pizza, and continued to roll over to a manhole cover, where one of the Ninja Turtles surfaced from the sewer, grabbed the pizza, and retreated back into his den.

The teacher observed that I had correctly demonstrated the elements of a fictional narrative. From that point on, I wanted to write fiction.

Of course, I was nine. Anything I was going to write was going to be derived from some sort of media I'd consumed. It didn't mean I couldn't be creative, but any writer knows that no matter what genre or subject you're approaching, you have to inject your work with personal experience.

At nine-years-old, most kids don't have enough life experience to write anything of much interest, aside from what they've seen in the movies. That's why most of the kids in our little fiction writing group could only write about the mundane experiences of everyday life.

I was unaware just how much media I had consumed by that point. Between slasher movies, ultraviolent video games and comic books, I should have had enough material to write a pretty stellar mixed-genre novel. My own Troma movie.

Little did I know that life was about to throw me a rough curve ball. I would finally have a life experience of my own that was worth writing about.

Lucky for you, you'll get to hear all about it in the next chapter.

CHAPTER 2:

How My @$$hole Brother Lit
My Parents' Bed on Fire

In the summer of 1992, my four-year-old brother, Jack, set my parents' bedroom on fire.

Earlier that year, my dad, an automotive technician for one of the big three, hurt his back at work. He was sleeping on the couch while I was off playing video games. It was a typically lazy summer day in the Sherman household.

Little did either of us know that in the next room, Jack had gotten hold of one of my dad's lighters.

I remember hearing the smoke detector going off, and the putrid smell of smoke as it wafted through the hallway and filled up the living room. It was suffocating.

Because of a recent back surgery, my dad couldn't get to Jack, so he yelled for me to grab him. I vaguely remember seeing my brother kneeling at the side of his own bed, a few of his brown hairs singed with ash. I don't know if I carried him out, pulled him, or just ran beside him. From what I heard later on, the door to Jack's room slammed shut just minutes after I got him out of there – and there wouldn't have been any way out if that happened.

The firefighters showed up as soon as we got to our front lawn. We lived across the street from a park, so everyone who was out barbequing ran to the curb to see what was going on. I remember feeling a bit frightened, but everything happened so fast that I didn't have time to digest it all. Within the hour, my mom was frantically pulling up to the house, and by this time, the black smoke was seeping outside. I didn't think I'd ever see the inside of our house again.

Jack and I spent the night at Janice Lovejoy's house. Everyone wanted to know what happened, but at that point, I didn't know Jack started the fire.

We stayed until the following night, when my mom picked us up and told us we'd be staying at the Holiday Inn until the insurance company could repair the damage.

It was a nice place, but what I got really excited about was that it had an indoor arcade. It actually had a *Teenage Mutant Ninja Turtles* cabinet. It would have been like having my own arcade for three months. However, the hotel had thirty floors, there was no front lawn, and we were going to be spending the next three months there. Not to mention, parking was a bitch. After a week, we relocated to the Residence Inn a few miles up the road.

The Residence Inn, rather than being located all in one cylindrical building, consisted of several structures surrounding an outdoor court and pool, which my parents liked because it gave us room to stretch our legs. Kids would play basketball there after school, and it even had an outdoor pool and jacuzzi. But I was still very much an indoors kid, who wanted nothing more than to play video games. Unfortunately, my Nintendo was one of many casualties, burnt to a cinder thanks to Jack and his lighter experiment.

One day, dad brought home a brand-new Nintendo, the one that came bundled with *Super Mario Bros. 3*. It didn't replace my previous library of 80 games, but I never had a copy of *Mario 3*, which normally meant I'd have to play it at the Lovejoys' house. Jack and I were ecstatic.

If you were a kid in the late 80's and early 90's, *Mario 3* needs no introduction. There was no better pastime than *Mario*

3. This was a really big game back in the day, with a lot of gameplay variety, eight really large levels, and it was pretty challenging.

But it also inspired me to pick up a pen and a notebook and write my first book. Yes, there in a small hotel suite, in the summer of '92, I penned my first novel. It wasn't *that* inspired – it was a novelization of *Super Mario 3*. Every chapter was literally based on an individual board from the game, and there wasn't much of a narrative. It read more like a strategy guide than a novel.

There wasn't much of a plot. It had Mario – and possibly Luigi, I don't remember – running from level to level, stomping goombas, avoiding piranha plants, and rescuing Princess Toadstool from Bowser Koopa (as I understood it, King Koopa now had a first name).

I didn't have a computer, so naturally, the only physical copy of the book got lost to the perils of time. Maybe I thought the book sucked, and I threw it out. Or maybe my mom was just doing some spring cleaning and tossed it in the trash. Maybe I gave it to this really cute maid I had a major crush on.

If I had to pick one thing I remember from my time at the Residence Inn, it was Nicole. She was twenty-two-years old, she had a real pretty face, with long, straight red hair, and she was really nice to me. It might have been because she was sympathetic to my family, knowing that we were going to be there for a number of months, but she wasn't just being kind for the sake of earning a paycheck.

One night, Nicole asked if I wanted to help her make her rounds. I was just another customer. I had no business following her around, helping her fold towels and things. But she asked, and to my surprise, my parents let me go. I'll be honest, I wasn't much help. I had a terrible work ethic at that age, and at one point, she told me she'd probably be better off if I just went back to my room. But there I was, helping her to make her rounds, talking to her about God knows what. I was just glad to be there with her.

To a nine-year-old kid with a huge crush on an amazingly attractive, older woman – who had then been asked out by said woman – this was a date. To my little exploding nine-year-old brain, this was a date. I had a twenty-two-year-old girlfriend. I was a stud.

And you can bet I bragged about it at Cub Scouts. My dad even backed me up. "Yep, he's got an older girlfriend," and he'd leave the rest of the details up to me.

Of course, it was just a fantasy. Obviously, Nicole wasn't trying to score points with me, and as I later found out, she had a real, honest-to-goodness boyfriend her own age. But she became a sincere friend during my stay, the older sister I never had. And while that may sound creepy, it was heartbreaking the day that we finally had to pack. My dad let me stay up past my bedtime, so that Nicole and I could work on a puzzle together. I remember that night fondly. The puzzle was the poster for *Indiana Jones and the Last Crusade*. I don't remember what we talked about, but I let her know that I would never forget her.

And I never did.

CHAPTER 3:

*Short Stories and That Rotten, No-
Good @%$! Horace Flanders*

T hat fall, I started fifth grade. At that point, I had a good
idea what I wanted to be when I grew up: a published
writer. I was heavily into Bruce Coville's My Teacher Is
an Alien series, a fascinating quadrilogy of young adult books
about aliens coming to Earth, dressing up as substitute teachers
and planning to conquer the world while the students tried to
stop them. The books were written in first-person, and each installment was told through the perspective of a different character.

I also liked the young adult horror novels, most famously
R.L. Stine's *Fear Street* series (sorry, but *Goosebumps* was a little
hokey to me). I read all four *Babysitter* books, not to mention
Silent Night. I was also a big fan of Alvin Schwartz's *Scary Stor-
ies to Tell in the Dark* series, compilations of grim folktales that
Schwartz expertly crafted into gothic short stories.

With little real-life experience to fuel my newfound creative hobby, I often looked for existing sources of inspiration.
One of my earliest inspirations was a cover to CRACKED magazine. I remember it vividly: a picture of Barney the purple dino-
saur clamped in the jaws of a T-Rex. The featured title: "Barney
Goes to Jurassic Park." I never read the actual comic strip, so I

was able to let my imagination take the reins. This was a high-concept idea. *Jurassic Park* was a huge movie at that time, and Jack was still young enough to watch Barney – which meant that I had to watch it, also. This was going to be my revenge.

I wrote the story in the span of a week, using an ancient word processor. I had one of those dot matrix printers that made a terrible grinding sound when you printed something off. I remember waking up at 4 in the morning, on a school day, to print it out so I could take it to class and show it off to the teacher.

The story had Barney working as an archaeologist, and he was taking his Backyard Gang to Jurassic Park so he could visit his ancestors – unaware that real dinosaurs don't actually sing and teach nursery rhymes. The genius of the book was that I included several of my classmates as characters. Most of them got maimed by vicious carnivores, but in my mind, they were all like the actors on a slasher movie set, anxious to see how gruesome their deaths were going to be.

And when Barney got his head bitten off by a tyranno-saur, the classroom cheered. I was a class hero, not only to the students, but to the teacher, who was impressed that a fifth-grader wrote something that actually *entertained*. I made an extra copy of it and set it out at reading time, so the students could read it at their leisure. Yeah, it was a bit pulpy, but it was a fun concept and it really got me excited to write more.

Then, I did what any big Hollywood studio does when a property does exceedingly well: I wrote a sequel.

Following in the footsteps of the original, CRACKED had another magazine cover, this one a little more macabre: it was a satirical picture of Superman – titled "Stuporman" – presented as a zombie. The title read: "Back from the Dead!" It was a parody of all the ways superheroes had risen from the grave. *The Death of Superman* was *the* comic book that got me interested in comics, and I also had the issue where Clark Kent was trying to return from the dead. I thought, how ridiculous could I make this sequel?

I started writing *Barney Goes to Jurassic Park 2: Back from the Grave*. In this installment, the survivors of Barney's Backyard Gang went to mourn their friend at his gravesite, when Barney rose from the dead as a murdering psychopath. Again, I included several students from the class. But this time, it didn't go over as well, for two reasons: one, it was more violent, which annoyed the teacher, despite the snickers of those who read it. When she read it out loud to the class, she had to actually omit a lot of things she deemed "too inappropriate."

Secondly, I think it offended some of the kids who were included. There was a kid named Justin who had a habit of farting in class. I'm sure it was embarrassing for him, but he couldn't help it – and I carried over his fatal flaw into the story. It was making fun of them rather than having fun with the concept. After that, I figured it was time to lay Barney to rest.

Occasionally, I was bullied. I was a white Jewish kid at a predominantly black school, and although most of my friends were black, that didn't mean that the bullies just left me alone. I got a few black eyes, and there were a number of times I was chased home by kids on bikes.

The bane of my existence was a kid named Horace Flanders, the son of one of my dad's best friends. We were in the same grade, in the same class, and he's what some would refer to as a *frenemy*. When he came over to my house, he played nice, but when our parents weren't around, he was a complete shithead.

At school, he made my life a living hell. He waited until I was done with my assignments, and when the teacher's back was turned, he tore up my papers. He bragged about having sex with older girls (although I don't think anyone believed him), and he thought he was good at martial arts because he saw a lot of kickboxing movies.

I hated the little fuck.

But where things began to escalate was when he started writing books himself – in which the teacher went to Jurassic Park.

This not only annoyed me, but everyone in class knew he

was ripping off my idea. We went back and forth, trying to one-up each other. After a while, I grew tired of writing sequels to someone else's knockoff of *my* knockoff, and so I went in a totally different direction: I wrote a science fiction trilogy.

There were three kids I hated more than anything in the whole world, and I dedicated one book to each of them. The first was Maddison Lovejoy, Mark Lovejoy's annoying older sister. I haven't talked a lot about her, but she was fat, she was a tattle-tale, and she was abusive. I almost didn't survive my stays at Janice Lovejoy's house because of her. She was always spying on me, letting Janice know if I was misbehaving or stepping out of line. She sat on me – those were fun times – and on one occasion, she even stuffed me in a sleeping bag, with my head toward the back of the bag, and zipped me up in it. I had no idea I was claustrophobic, and that is *not* a way you want to find out.

Then there was Cedar Ramirez, a Latino kid who always chased me home on his bike. He wasn't much of a bully, but we hated each other, and there was a girl I had a crush on who I think liked him more than she liked me.

Of course, there was Horace Flanders, the paper-ripping, sex-obsessed, story-stealing, whiny little mama's boy who made my life a living Hell until the day I moved away from Oak Park schools. The three of these kids all became the major antagonists in my new wave of science fiction books, in which each kid was an alien who invaded my school, and I had to convince everyone to stop them. Because I used their real names, these books were distributed in limited quantities.

Strangely enough, Horace and I partnered up on a comic strip. Neither one of us knew how to draw (Horace bragged that he did, but I say otherwise), and we knew next to nothing about creating comic books. We used color pens, for one thing, and the stories never had any context. They were just ugly looking dudes fighting each other.

The Death of Superman was unique in that, the entire issue was drawn using splash pages – each page was its own panel. It was a technique the artists used to make the action seem more dramatic, and the stakes higher. However, I tended to adapt this style to all of my early comics, out of laziness rather than necessity.

Horace created a character called *Cook Man*, a psychotic chef-turned-serial killer who butchered and ate his victims. So, in Cook Man's wake, I created *Cook Boy*. It would only seem natural to assume that Cook Boy was just a lame knock-off of other superhero sidekicks, like Superboy and Batgirl. But I turned Cook Boy into its own thing, long after Horace gave up on comics. Cook Boy was an anti-hero who delved deep into the trenches of Hell to fight off evil forces. Each issue pitted the title character against a different demon. There was no story. Essentially, each issue had Cook Boy talking smack to whatever villain I had him go up against.

Cook Boy had a unique look – not out of necessity, but because I couldn't draw. A lot of the classic depictions of Superman and Batman featured characters with squared jaws and lots of muscles. Having no idea how to draw in that style, I ended up giving Cook Boy a square head, with slanted triangles for eyes and a bandanna like a ninja. He also had a giant, curved knife-blade grafted on his right arm, and a pitchfork on the other. The comics involved the character impaling enemies using these tools, before going up against the big, bad evildoer in the final pages.

There were other comics I created right up until sixth grade, although by this time I was leaving the artwork up to the computer. Yes, even at the dawn of the 90's, computers could be used for art, but it was primitive stuff, and Photoshop was a long way off.

I used a piece of software called *Comic Book Creator*, which came loaded with pre-drawn characters, backgrounds, and layouts. There wasn't a ton of variety in terms of page layouts, but there was a good selection of effects and word bubbles to choose from. However, because the software was so limited, I lost interest quickly, and by the time I was halfway through the sixth grade, my comic book career ended.

CHAPTER 4:

Junior High is Full of @$&!ing Twats

For the remainder of grade school, I attended Berkley schools, which contained a larger Jewish population. I had a hard time adjusting because I didn't jive with the other kids. My friends at the Oak Park schools watched Power Rangers. Were we a little old for that show? Maybe. But we loved it, and even in the sixth grade, we'd be out on the playground, screaming, "It's morphin' time!" Then we'd pretend to beat each other's asses until math started.

But god forbid I mention my love of Amy Jo Johnson at Norup Middle School. I had a hard time finding common ground with these kids. Even the things I realized they were into – like video games – immediately turned into a nail in my coffin if I even mentioned the word "game" to any of them. I know kids can be cruel, but you'd think all a kid like me had to do was find a group of kids as anti-social as me to hang out with, and I couldn't find one.

Some kids just have the bad luck of being "that kid" – that unfortunate soul who sits in the far corner of the classroom, his back to the rest of his classmates while he gets spitballed to death. At times, I felt like I was that kid. I just had an active imagination.

At that point, I was WAY big into *Mortal Kombat,* an

immensely popular, ultra-violent arcade game released by Midway, and which had become the subject of heated debate revolving around violent video games. This was around the time when the media blamed everything on rock music, violent video games, and television. A kid sets his grandparents on fire, and who's to blame? Beavis and Butt-head.

Despite all the televised hoopla about video games corrupting the minds of the young – which Socrates was accused of, as well, if you know your history – I was a *Mortal Kombat* addict. Or, as one kid referred to me as, a *Mortal Kombat* freak. I spent more time ripping off the heads of my enemies than I ever did reading a book or drawing a comic. I had a strategy guide for each game, and I spent hours practicing the special moves and improving my game.

There was a character named Baraka, a mutant from the realm of Outworld whose features included a bald head, gnarly sharp teeth, and large spikes that protruded from each of his arms. One time in class, I rolled up two pieces of loose-leaf paper and stuck one in each of my fists – I was Baraka. I started imagining that I was doing his famous "shredding" move, where he swung his arms up and down. Heaven help you if you were on the receiving end of that – you would jump right into the attack, creating a bloody massacre as Baraka shredded you on his blades.

Some of the other kids saw me doing that and laughed at me. They didn't ask, "Hey, who are you trying to be?", or "Hey, can I join in?" I understand why I had problems making friends. If you're sitting in class, minding your own business, when all of a sudden, some weird new kid starts swinging his arms around with two pieces of rolled up paper jutting out from his fists, are *you* going to be inclined to make friends with him?

But it goes to show just how different the culture was at this new school. I remember my first day there. A kid named Alec Burkovich offered to show me around. It was in-between classes, so the hallway was crowded with students. As I started following this kid through the halls, he started weaving his way through students until he lost me. It was no big deal, the class-rooms all had their numbers above their doors, but it was a dick move.

So, I kept to myself. For the rest of that year, I didn't make any new friends. I just did my homework, went home, and played video games. What else was I supposed to do? No one wanted to hang out with me. So, fuck 'em.

During my self-imposed exile, I started working on a new book called *Life After Death*. It shared quite a few elements from *Cook Boy*. All I remember about it was that the protagonist was murdered, and he came back to life to avenge himself. It was this weird combination of goth fantasy and C.S. Lewis – writer of the *Narnia* books. I followed it up with a sequel, and when I showed them to my Language Arts teacher, she was impressed, and al-lowed some of the other kids to give them a read.

By this point, my writing became darker, reflecting my newfound moodiness at this new school. I hated it there. The kids were jerks, the teachers didn't seem to pay attention, and I spent a lot of my time talking to my guidance counselor, who wasn't a big help and only made me look like more of a nut bar to the other kids. At one point, she thought I might be suicidal. I didn't want to kill myself, I just wanted to make some friends. Being alone sucks.

This was also the first time I was given homework over the summer. Yeah, imagine that. I had to read a novel and do a project based on it. Whoop-di-fuckin'-doo.

The book I chose was Lois Duncan's suspense novel, *I Know What You Did Last Summer*. This was a few years before the movie with Jennifer Love Hewitt. One of the projects was to write a continuation of the novel. From what I remember of the book, it was more of a murder-mystery than a straight-up slasher, which was what my sequel became. When I finished it, it came in at somewhere between 15 and 20 pages, which may not seem like a lot, as far as novels go. But for a thirteen-year-old doing an assignment over the summer – not too shabby.

When seventh grade began, my new Language Arts

teacher flipped through the pages, saying, "Well, you definitely get an 'A' for effort." That was just great. She probably didn't even read the fucking thing. I could've probably just taken fifteen sheets of paper and typed "AAAAAAAAAAAAAAAAAAAAAA" from front to back.

If I'm starting to sound bitter, seventh grade was even worse than sixth. I couldn't get along with anyone. Everything I did, I got made fun of for. If my hair was too fluffy, I had a Jewfro. If I gelled my hair back, I was too preppy. If I wore corduroys, I was out of style. If I wore blue jeans, I was trying too hard to be like everyone else. I couldn't win for losing.

What really hurt my confidence was when I mustered up the courage to ask out a girl, Jenny Friedburg. I had a crush on Jenny since first semester, and while we occasionally talked, we weren't close. We were barely even acquaintances. We had gym together, and once in a while, I might say, "Hi, how ya doing?" My dad worked on her mother's computer a few times, so that was my "in," I guess.

When I asked her out, everyone in the seventh grade made this big deal about it. I don't even remember telling anyone that I was going to ask her. So, when I caught up with her and asked her out on a date, why were we suddenly surrounded by twenty of our peers? Because we were in seventh grade, that's why.

It was like an episode of *Dawson's Creek*. She said she'd have to think about it, which left everyone surrounding us wondering whether or not they should tune in for *Part II* of *Lenny's Shitty-Ass Life*.

Well, we ended up going on the date. Her mom drove us to the movies, and unfortunately, I was a gentleman, so I let her pick the flick. The movie was *Clueless*, starring Alicia Silverstone ("as if!"). While we were in the theater, we ran into another couple from school, and before I could say anything, Jenny was whisking me down the aisle. "Hurry, before they see us," she whispered. At that point, I was so glad to be on the date with her, that I didn't care that she was ashamed to be seen with me in public.

I cared the next day.

In gym class, I told her what a fun time I had, which was the only nice thing I could really say, given how bad the movie was.

"What are you talking about?"

"You know, the date. I just had a really good time. We should do it again, sometime."

I have a feeling that even if she wasn't around her friends, her reaction would have been exactly the same. "First of all, let me get one thing straight – that *wasn't* a date. And second, we saw each other at the movies – it's not like we went together."

As if.

Her mom only drove us there and drove us back. It wasn't like she decided to pick me up on the side of the road out of pity.

As she ran past me, I heard one of her friends go, "What a loser."

That was the highlight of my day.

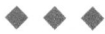

Rather than push myself to make friends, to blend in, to ask more girls out on dates – which is what I should have fucking done in the first place – I became even more of a social shut-in. I didn't want to talk to anybody. Just go home, do my fucking homework, sit in a corner by myself and watch *Power Rangers* until I cried myself to sleep. And even then, the show was absolute shit because all of the best characters left – even Amy Jo Johnson. Life in the seventh grade was complete and utter garbage.

I continued to write stories whenever I could, but by this time, my mood was so dark and I was so removed from everything around me, that the stories just reflected that. And a lot of the time, they took large leaps of faith. I wrote a story where a kid got AIDS – a kid who, like me, wasn't even sexually active – and then went around school pissed off all the time because he was going to die.

Hell, I even plagiarized. I wrote a prison story about two guys who became friends during their incarceration, and eventually, years later, they both get out and reunite with one another. And one of the characters' names was Blue. Sound familiar? My Language Arts teacher called me on it right away, saying it sounded too much like *The Shawshank Redemption*, which had come out the year before. I explained to her that it really wasn't ripping off *Shawshank*, but that in fact it was just a really edgy sequel to Nick Jr.'s *Blue's Clues*.

Yeah, she didn't buy it.

CHAPTER 5:

My First Space Opera, and My Junior High Woes

That same year, the Star Wars trilogy was re-released to video. Surprisingly, before those tapes came out, I never knew what George Lucas looked like. Suddenly, there he was, being interviewed by film critic Leonard Maltin. This was a game changer for me, for several reasons. Most people remember these interviews as the first time Lucas shed light on his upcoming prequel trilogy. But for me, it was the first time I realized that people could earn a living making movies. People were out there every day, creating special effects, recording sounds, photographing moving images that would later be spliced together and projected in a movie theater in front of thousands of people.

I always thought you had to be rich to make a movie like *Star Wars* – or any movie, for that matter. Normal, regular, everyday people couldn't make movies. In 1995, this might have been true. Technology has come a long way, hasn't it?

In that interview, Lucas discussed the struggles he endured in order to make those movies. But he also touched on the inspiration for returning to the franchise, and what fueled him to tell the backstories of a lot of his original characters. He described the original three movies as the *redemption* of Anakin

Skywalker, a man we hardly know anything about because he spends all three movies brooding in a mask and black cape. The three new movies he was preparing to make were going to be *about* Anakin Skywalker, and how he fell from grace, becoming the most iconic movie villain of all time.

It was a story that hadn't been told yet.

In that moment, I knew I wanted to write a science fiction trilogy. I wanted to write the equivalent of the *Star Wars* trilogy, but as novels. There was this whole side of *Star Wars* that hadn't been explored, and if I could create my own worlds, and my own characters, I could write something that was maybe better than *Star Wars*. It was my turn to finally put my name on the map. I was only thirteen years old, but damn it, I was going to be the youngest published writer ever – or at least in the metro-Detroit area.

Not long after I watched that interview between Maltin and Lucas, I began work on the *Galactic Redemption* trilogy.

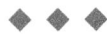

Galactic Redemption told the story of young farm boy, Jake Houston, who aspired to leave his tiny, insignificant swamp planet in order to do battle against a tyrannical dictator. In the course of his journey, Jake met up with an aged wizard, a cocky pirate and his muscular gargoyle co-pilot in order to thwart the galaxy's evil forces, only to realize that the evil emperor was none other than – drum roll please – Jake's long-lost brother!

Yeah, it was a blatant *Star Wars* knockoff.

I honestly never intended to plagiarize. My original idea was to write a story about a man who descends into darkness, even though his original intentions are good. That was the arc of Anakin Skywalker, the part of *Star Wars* that hadn't been told yet. I wanted to get there first.

What ended up happening was, I wrote myself into the same corner that most young, inexperienced writers trap themselves in. Rather than using my own experiences, which were few and far between, I took what I saw in the movies and pretended it was my own. Growing up, Stephen King was a huge fan of J.R.R. Tolkien, but he intentionally stayed away from the fantasy genre because he knew all about this particular beginner's trap. King eventually developed his own style in writing masterpieces like *The Gunslinger* and *The Stand*, but there were occasional nods to Tolkien in his works. Still, Stephen King was paying homage – and little did I know, I was stealing.

It wasn't hidden that well, either. The names of the characters and the planets all changed, but I stuck to the traditional Earth-bound locations. I had a desert planet, a swamp planet, even a forest planet. For fuck's sakes, this was literature. I could have come up with any environment I wanted. Instead, I was writing with a budget.

I passed the story around to a few classmates, who all pointed out that it was ripping off the most popular space fantasy film in history.

Despite this setback, I continued the story with *The Search for the Galactic Redemption*. In this installment, Jake discovered that the sexy princess character he met in the first book was actually his sister, and she had a boyfriend who – surprise, surprise – became the villain. Jake continued his training with the old man to further his skills as a galactic warrior – I didn't have any special title for him – before once again confronting the evil emperor in the last act. This one was weird, because there was a pointless scene in which Jake built a robot who could mimic everyone's voices, and I didn't follow through with this scene. You never see the robot again. Also, during Jake's training, the old wizard pitted him against a giant scorpion. While Jake battled the scorpion with his galactic blade – basically, a sword – the weapon changed colors, with each color symbolizing a different skill. Again, I only used that detail in that one scene, and it never showed up again. Maybe I should have written another draft.

The third installment, and the conclusion to my epic

trilogy, was the strangest case yet. There were two versions, each with a completely different final act – not to mention, the titles were different. The first iteration was called *Return to the Planet,* and had Jake returning to his home planet after he thought it had been destroyed in the first book. He then learned that the emperor was using a secret weapon, dubbed the Genesis project – you see where I'm going with this? – that could replicate entire planets. At that point, I was well aware that these stories had become disappointing knockoffs of the *Star Wars* trilogy, and so now I was calling attention to it, breaking the fourth wall by having the characters acknowledge that the villain was using plots from old movies to try and ensnare his enemies. It was a lazy attempt to wrap up my trilogy. It was a cop out, as if I was saying, "Oh yeah, I totally meant to rip off *Star Wars* the whole time."

I hated that ending, so shortly after I wrapped up that project, I rewrote the final act, and changed the title to *From Hero to Galactic Knight* – equally as lazy. In this iteration, the setup was the same, except Jake and the other characters fought a final battle on a forest planet, where they teamed up with its primitive inhabitants, a tribe of cannibalistic primitives called Snipers. To top it off, when Jake won the battle and defeated the emperor once and for all, he pursued a romantic relationship – with his sister. George R. R. Martin, eat your heart out.

The whole trilogy reeked of a poor man's version of *Star Wars*, and the worst part was, I firmly believed that I copied all of Lucas's mistakes, rather than all the things he got right. *Star Wars* was a personal story for Lucas, who talked about characters escaping from their everyday lives to venture into the unknown. This was a trope he used in not only *Star Wars*, but in his first feature, *THX 1138*. In many ways, this was something Lucas had to do himself, when he decided to break through the confines of the tiny farming community of Modesto in order to enter the filmmaking industry.

If anything, I should have written about a kid who couldn't break out of his surroundings, no matter how hard he tried, because he didn't have any control over his life – the reality for most teenagers. Even as the kid looked around and saw what other people were doing all around him, he wouldn't have been able to break free.

In those days, as not only an aspiring writer, but an arrogant one, I was concerned with emulating success, and copying what others had done, as opposed to venturing off and finding my own story. The other thing that hurt *Galactic Redemption* – not to mention most of my writing at that age – was, there was no real motivation. Why was Jake fighting against the emperor? Why would an old man, who was unrelated to any of the other characters, and who had very little connection with their pasts, offer to help Jake in the first place? Why did the emperor want control of the galaxy? In my stories, the emperor was always portrayed as monitoring the galaxy from his hidden fortress – a fortress that everyone knew about, apparently – and he always had a single henchman to carry out his evil deeds. What if in *Star Wars*, the galaxy was only ruled by Darth Vader, and there were no Stormtroopers to carry out his bidding? It would make for pretty lame storytelling.

Despite being unsatisfied with the final result, I tried to make some money off of my work. It had been my dream, ever since I started writing in the fourth grade, to be a published writer. How cool would it be to walk into Borders one day, and see something I created sitting in the storefront window? I always envisioned myself surrounded by fans at a book signing. I wasn't even thinking about the money, at that time. But I figured, why not?

At the tail end of junior high, I took a course in journalism, writing for the school paper. I really wanted to head the movies section, but probably because I was just too obsessed with movies, I was charged with writing other types of articles. As one of the monthly issues was going to press, I asked the teacher if I could run off copies of the entire *Galactic Redemption* trilogy, and sell them – at two dollars a pop. As you might have guessed, I had no business sense whatsoever. I grabbed one of my classmates so he could help me run five copies of each book – that was well over 500 pieces of paper. At one point, the secretary asked who was going to pay for it all.

"Just bill the journalism department," I replied.

Despite selling the books at less than bargain-bin price, they were not well-received – meaning, I didn't sell a single copy. And I got scolded for wasting ink and paper on the school's dime.

◆ ◆ ◆

That was also the year I met Jessie Cunningham and became best friends with Jerry Breckinfield.

I knew Jerry since the day I started at Norup. Like all the other kids, he didn't like me. I knew he didn't like me because when I sat next to him in music class on that first day, he immediately gave me a dirty look, packed up his books and sat at the other end of the classroom. That entire period, he just stared at me, with this scornful, pissed-off look. I never talked to Jerry, but that image of him staring me down like a bull in heat was engraved in my brain for all of junior high.

That was until one day, at the beginning of eighth grade, he came in wearing a black Boba Fett t-shirt. We had Language Arts together – which doubled as our journalism class – and even though we didn't share many classes over the years, I remembered back to that first day of school, and I made sure to keep my distance.

On that day, he noticed that I wore a black Darth Vader shirt. He walked up to me, and I realized his walk was a little abnormal. I didn't realize until later that he had pigeon toe, a condition where one of your feet tilts slightly in at an angle. I also noticed that he wore shabby clothes – nothing out of the dumpster, but obviously hand-me-downs, a lot of baggy torn jeans and Christmas sweaters.

He walked over to me, this kid who never said more than

one word to me, and looked me up and down. "So… you going to see the Special Editions when they come out?"

I didn't know how to react. I was trembling – this kid scared me. I subconsciously avoided this kid all throughout junior high. Then I thought, he wouldn't be talking to me if he still had this huge problem with me. What's he going to do, punch me in the face if I tell him no?

"Yeah, definitely," I said, almost wanting to duck because I thought he really might hit me.

"So, uh… who's your favorite *Star Wars* character?"

I paused. Well, I had to think about it. I didn't really have a…

"Luke, I suppose," I blurted out. What a dumb response. No one's favorite character is Luke. He's like the everyman of the *Star Wars* saga. Everyone relates to him because he's the least interesting character, and yet the entire trilogy is *about* him.

"So, uh… you play video games?"

You get the gist. We spent the whole period ignoring our teacher's lesson on conjugating verbs and getting to know each other better. We even walked home together. It turned out that we only lived a few blocks away from each other. I finally asked him why, on that day three years before, he acted the way he had. I was frightened of the answer, especially because I was still on my guard. I thought maybe he was just messing with me this whole time, mocking my love of *Star Wars* so he could get more fuel to pick on me with.

"Because all the other kids said you were an asshole."

That first day attending classes at Norup, I said less than five words to anyone. I spent most of the day trying not to throw up. I had never been "the new kid" before, so it was a terrible experience. And aside from that jerk-off, Alec Berkovich, intentionally getting me lost in the hallways, a lot of the other kids blatantly told me not to try to be friends with them. As I said – kids can be cruel.

"Well, I'm not," I said defensively.

"Yeah, I know that now."

Jerry and I were very much alike, but we were also very different. We both loved *Star Wars* and video games, and the funny thing was, neither of us was that competitive. We didn't really like playing games against each other – unless it was *Mortal Kombat*, in which case, after he saw how skilled I was, didn't like playing against me in that game, either. Jerry also had an incredible fondness for comic books. He could actually draw. Not draw as in, check out this week's issue of *Cook Boy,* draw – he knew how to *draw*. At that point, I still had a few issues of *Cook Boy* that I hadn't thrown in the trash, and I let him look at them so he could critique them. And boy, was he honest – almost to a crippling degree. He analyzed every line, every muscle, every word bubble. It was as if Stan Lee were instructing a five-year-old how to draw comic books.

But I respected him for that. He didn't help me become a better artist – why help the competition, after all – but I appreciated his ability to not care about my feelings for the sake of critiquing art – or lack thereof.

But as it turned out, Jerry also came from a somewhat broken home. He didn't talk much about it. In fact, the whole time we knew each other, I only saw the inside of his house once.

For starters, Jerry's dad was diagnosed with cancer, and from what little he spoke about his dad, he seemed to get the raw end of the stick. It wasn't so much that his parents were abusive – neglectful was a better word. He had a younger sister, who seemed to be the apple of their eye. Understandably, cancer can bring out the worst in a person. But his dad would say things like, "Can you outrun a bullet, son?"

On occasion, even my dad contracted diarrhea of the mouth. Ever since he hurt his back and went on disability, he became increasingly irritable, impatient, and it got to the point where he couldn't say a nice word about anyone. But it seemed that for all the shit my dad put me through, somehow, Jerry had it slightly worse. It made sense that he wanted to spend a lot of his afternoons at my house, playing video games and talking about movies.

◆ ◆ ◆

And then there was Jessie.

Jessie Cunningham moved to Oak Park from Pontiac, and this was her first year at Norup – lucky her. Ever since the Jenny Friedburg incident, I was cautious about talking to girls. But I was attracted to Jessie from the moment I met her. We had two classes with each other, gym and personal development, and in both classes, she sat close to me. It took a few weeks to actually muster up the courage to even make eye contact with her. In fact, she was the one who initiated the conversation. And it was all because I wouldn't stop staring at her.

"You have some kind of problem with me?"

"No," I said, in a timid voice.

"Then why do you keep looking at me?"

"Sorry," was all I could say.

Then one day, she slipped me a note at the end of class. It was that simple. She slipped me a note and before I could even open it, she left.

It read: "Do you like me?"

It was a simple question, but teenagers are not direct about their feelings for one another. It's all a series of passing notes, whispering to your friends in the hallways, and asking your friends to ask the girl's friends if she likes you. I never experienced someone who was so direct.

The next day I caught up with her at her locker. "I have a hard time talking to you," I said, which was how I honestly felt.

"Why?"

"Girls make me feel uncomfortable."

"What, are you gay or something?"

"No, I just have a hard time talking to girls."

"Oh. So… do you like me?"

"Yeah… I guess so," I said. I never felt so vulnerable. But

that was it – I was somehow telling her how I honestly felt. I thought, *this must be what it's like to have a meaningful conversation with a member of the opposite sex.*

"You don't have to be shy to talk to me," she said. "Truth is, I think you're interesting. I'm new here, and I'm looking to make as many friends as I can." I recalled how hard it was for me to make friends when I started. Even then, the only friend I really had was Jerry, and we just started hitting it off earlier that year.

"Well... I'll be your friend, then," I said.

And for the rest of that semester, we were.

◆ ◆ ◆

Jessie was unlike any girl I'd ever met. For one, she was big into the Detroit Red Wings. In the mid-90's, Detroit was going through this big sports renaissance. I never liked sports, but it was impossible to ignore all the hype surrounding the Red Wings, who were about to take home their first Stanley Cup win since 1955. Even kids who typically didn't like sports shared in the excitement.

She was a teenage girl, so she fancied Backstreet Boys and N'Sync. But Jessie was essentially a tomboy. She wore ripped jeans and baggie sweatshirts – not out of necessity, like with Jerry, but because that was her style.

A lot of times, we took walks around the block, and she told me about where she used to live, her old friends, and her family. Unlike Jerry, where you had to really dig just to find out his home address, Jessie was an open book.

As it turned out, Jessie seemed to be attracted to the wrong type. Within weeks, she began hanging out with a bad crowd. They smoked cigarettes, and a couple of them did drugs – they were a group I typically didn't associate with. So, Jessie would divide her time between hanging out with them and with me.

It was only a matter of time before Jessie started dating one of these kids – Peter Jenkins, this blond, froofy-haired, pin-headed prick I knew from Sunday school. I didn't see the attraction, but I knew that I didn't have an icy chance in hell of being with her. I didn't think she liked me in that way, and I wasn't going to risk our newfound friendship by delving into those waters.

Then one day, I sat at a table with Peter in personal development. Jessie hadn't been in class for a couple of days. Peter was carrying on, acting like a class clown, being his usual jerk-off self, when he dropped a random bomb about Jessie. It was me, Peter, and a third kid, Kyle Brennan. We were trying to stave off boredom, when Peter mentioned that Jessie, "the new girl," was having sex.

I guess it's reasonable to expect that a lot of kids start having sex in their teens. That's why they teach sex education in the seventh grade. And I guess I could understand if teens started when they were sixteen, but fourteen just seemed too young. And I knew Jessie was a tomboy, but as open as she was about her past, I figured she would have brought that up.

Kyle let his curiosity get the best of him. "With who?"

Peter leaned in. "With me."

Kyle slammed his hand down on the table. "Shut the hell up!"

Peter was so proud of himself. He lost his virginity to this girl, and took hers, as well. It made me question her moral compass, but then I realized, Jessie would have told me – and Peter was the kind of asshole who *would* lie about something like that.

As it turned out, Jessie was quickly becoming a school urban legend. She was gone for several weeks at that point, and when I went to her house to see where she'd been, her parents wouldn't tell me. But in school, her "friends" started to talk openly about her sexual promiscuity, suicide attempts, and where she had been for the past weeks: at a juvenile detention center, for assaulting her parents. I even saw one kid sketch a picture of Jessie stabbing herself repeatedly. It was horrifying and in complete bad taste – the kind of thing I was used to seeing at that school.

None of these things resembled the girl I had hung out with. That was until one day, after about a month went by, that she showed up at my doorstep. We went for a walk, and she told me that she was, in fact, serving time at a juvenile detention center. She suffered from bipolar disorder, and even though she was on medication for it, her parents couldn't deal with her violent mood swings. Her parents had Jessie later in life, so they were up there in age, and they couldn't defend themselves against her physical outbreaks.

I was completely taken off-guard, but I also realized that I didn't spent as much time with her as I would have liked. She was trying to make the right kinds of friends, and she figured she couldn't do that by being honest about this darker side of her personality.

Deep down, I was flattered that she trusted me enough to come out with the truth. I asked her about her and Peter, which she quickly denied – at first. The thing was, Jessie wasn't a virgin. In fact, she lost her virginity two years earlier, to a childhood friend back home. Being the sheltered kid that I was, I asked her a little more about her sexual past. She explained that she wasn't a slut, that she was faithful to her boyfriends, but that she was just experimental, and that her parents couldn't always keep an eye on her, so she sometimes took advantage of the situation. She had since broken things off with Peter, because he was going around school spreading stories about her that no one had the right to know. That didn't mean she was single, though – she met a boy in juvie, and they were building a relationship despite being separated by gender.

It turned out that Jessie was going to spend the rest of the semester in juvie. They had educational services there, but the quality didn't match up with that of a normal public school. Jessie made a conscious decision to repeat the eighth grade the following year, which meant she wouldn't be going to high school with me. It bummed me out, but again, I respected her for making the right decision. She was trying to better her situation.

We spent time together over the summer, and to fill in the gaps when she wasn't around, I always had Jerry, who came over to watch movies or play Nintendo 64. The recurring theme of our conversations was girls we liked, but I was always fixated on Jessie. Our tastes in girls were different: he seemed to like the skinny girls, the ones who didn't share the public spotlight. I was the complete opposite: I went for the girls who were completely out of my league. But Jessie was the first *girl* friend I had, and truth be told, my feelings only grew stronger. Not only did we get along, but I was extremely attracted to her. But every time I saw her, she had a boyfriend. And I was too much of a chicken shit to make my move.

CHAPTER 6:

Growing Pains and Speech Class

High school started, and at first, things didn't get much easier. The fucking kids started in on me right away. If they didn't like me, or didn't jive with me, they would announce it publicly in front of the class. I never understood what it was about me that drew that kind of reaction from people. I wasn't a particularly abnormal looking kid – a little anti-social, maybe even a little overweight, but so what? There were a lot of fat kids who had friends, so it couldn't have been my physical appearance. As far as my clothes, I wasn't trending with the latest fashions, but I basically wore jeans and a t-shirt. What was it about me that projected the word "loser"?

I tried hanging out with Jessie as much as I could, but by the time she got out of juvie, she made a whole new group of friends. Thankfully, her new clique seemed to be a healthier bunch, and I was happy for her. But as time passes, especially as a teenager, you start to resent change.

Then one night, Jessie came to my house and stayed until it was dark out. It was awkward, because I noticed she kept staring at me. We were friends for a little more than a year, and as much as I still liked her, I put a pin in my feelings because she always had a boyfriend, and she never showed any interest in me.

As I walked her home that night, she finally admitted

what I hoped to hear from her since the day I met her. She told me she had feelings for me.

You would think this was good news. But as much as I talked to Jerry about going out with girls and was tired of the constant rejections, I never considered what would happen if one of them said that they *liked* me.

This was a delicate situation, because Jessie was a friend. To suddenly be all gushy around each other would have made things awkward. And believe it or not, I wasn't thinking, *Hey, I might lose my virginity to this girl.* I cared about her so much that I didn't want to ruin things. As much as I wanted this, as soon as she told me how she felt, I kept my distance.

In Language Arts, we were reading the works of Mr. William Shakespeare, who I loved ever since I started studying him in the sixth grade, before I even switched schools. We were reading *Romeo & Juliet,* of all things, and it was the first time I'd heard the term "star-crossed lovers" – two people who are destined to be together, but are kept apart by circumstances beyond their control.

I fed her some stupid bullshit about star-crossed lovers. The truth was, I was too nervous to say that I wanted to be her boyfriend. It took me years, maybe even decades, to realize it, but I was not mentally ready to be in a relationship with a girl. And while I think things would have been fine if we *had* dated, I'm not quite sure we would have ended up together. I don't know. I never really got any closure out of it.

Not a happy kind of closure, anyway.

Despite her attempts, I decided it would be best if Jessie and I just remained friends. I know it was probably one of the dumbest decisions I made. I had every reason to man up and become the next love of her life. But it was an experience I never had. No girl ever told me they had a crush on me. Jessie even tried to kiss me, and I shied away from her. God, was I a fucking moron?

But sometimes, life has a funny way of getting even, of reminding you of the kinds of choices you make and sticking them right back in your face.

Two weeks after I turned her down, her and Jerry started going out.

The worst part was, both of them asked for my consent before they started seeing each other. They weren't hiding anything behind my back, they were being the courteous friends that I grew to know and respect. They cared about my feelings.

And like the scared dipshit that I was, I said I was fine with it.

Then the jealousy set in.

First of all, ever since Jessie revealed that she wasn't a virgin, she started telling me every time her and a boyfriend would do stuff together. Most times, I lived vicariously through her, but this was my two best friends. I started to resent Jerry most of all, because all the crazy stuff they were doing together, I wanted that to be me and her.

The more time that passed, the more jealous I got. While their frequent displays of affection weren't appropriate, I ended up driving both of them away. It got to the point where I started to think hateful thoughts about them. They wouldn't even come over to my house together. By the end of freshman year, our friendship had all but deteriorated.

The straw that broke the camel's back was when I went around school referring to Jessie as a slut. I was suddenly one of those assholes spreading rumors about her. One of her friends overheard me, and before I knew it, Jessie confronted me.

"Have you been going around calling me names behind my back?"

"Yeah," I said. "You have to understand, I've been so angry about how this all worked out. You should be with me. Not him."

"Thanks for being honest with me," Jessie said. "But I don't think we can be friends anymore."

Not surprisingly, a few weeks later, Jessie and Jerry broke up. Jessie went on with her life, as if I was never a part of it. I saw her around the school hallways, but she never even made eye contact. I didn't exist to her.

As for Jerry, the little we saw of each other, it was like that first day at Norup. He hated me. This one time, we shared math together. He sat a few desks in front of me. As the class was passing back graded tests to each other, Jerry glanced at my paper, then turned to me with this real nasty grin, and gave me the finger. In junior high, I guess I was known for being an over-achiever, but in high school, as the work became more challenging, my grades started to slip a bit. This was his way of telling me to eat shit.

As the semester drew to a close, I stopped seeing Jerry at school at all. Some of the kids he normally hung out with said they saw him on the streets in raggedy clothes, begging for drugs. The last I heard, he dropped out of school to look for work. I never saw or heard from him again.

❖ ❖ ❖

I don't remember feeling as numb as I did freshman year of high school. I lost my two best friends. As far as the rest of the kids, it never got as bad as it was in middle school, but the bullies were still plentiful. And we now had classes that combined all the grades together, so of course, the upperclassmen had to have their fun.

A lot of kids at that point would have turned to drugs or alcohol. As I've been saying, I was sheltered. I had no idea where to score pot, and I never acquired a taste for booze. So, I turned to the next best thing: comedy.

The two big comedians back then were George Carlin and Chris Rock, both with these huge specials that aired on HBO. I knew George Carlin from his stint as Rufus in the *Bill & Ted* movies, and more shockingly, I remembered him as Mr. Conductor on *Thomas the Tank Engine*. I had no idea, before seeing *Back in Town*, his 1996 comedy special, that he was best known for his stand-up. As a kid, I saw acts like Eddie Murphy and Andrew Dice Clay, and I was turned off by them, because all I heard was the swearing. I was too young to get the jokes.

Chris Rock just released *Bring the Pain*. Rock was known for a few movies, but this was before he played Marty the zebra in the *Madagascar* films.

These guys cracked me up. I watched Carlin's performances repeatedly, taping them whenever they aired on TV, and then I'd go back to school to do some of his act in front of my classmates. It seemed to lift some of the drabness. I had problems getting along with the older kids, but some of the ones I went to middle school with had grown up a little, and they were a little more tolerant. I enjoyed making them laugh, even if I was copying someone else.

During Freshman year, I signed up for speech class. Not a class where they correct your speech impediment – a class geared toward writing and delivering speeches. This was one of those classes with students from all four grades. Because I was shy, and I was still perfecting my George Carlin-isms, sometimes I would blurt out stuff that was just – well, stupid. And the seniors weren't shy about telling me to close my bear trap.

This was when I decided, I'd be damned if I was going to go through another four years as a doormat for these fucking kids.

For our first speech, we had to talk about our pet peeves. Our teacher, a big but quirky woman named Ms. Palmer, was grading us on our writing skills (no problem for me), as well as our vocal inflections, our use of fillers ("ums" and "you knows"), and our overall performance. Did we stay behind the podium for the entire speech, or did we get out in front of the class and move our hands around, like we cared about what we were presenting?

I don't know what it was, but at that moment, I didn't care what the kids thought of me. They were going to make fun of me no matter what I said or did, so why not turn a few heads? The speech was primarily composed of my words, but I sprinkled in a little George Carlin and Chris Rock for good measure.

I talked about drugs, drive-by shootings, and at one point, for no apparent reason, I slapped myself in the face as I used one of Rock's famous quotes: "Don't vote for crack, vote for smack!" It was like watching a stand-up comedian do his act. I went on a random tangent. I rehearsed it at home dozens of times, but nothing prepared me for getting up in front of my classmates, many of them students I didn't get along with, and delivering this speech.

When I finished, I got a standing ovation. I think I even got an A on the speech, for my ability to interact directly with my audience.

But I think what impressed Ms. Palmer the most was, she saw this shy kid come out of his shell within seconds of getting up in front of the class. From that moment on, I made some friends.

It got to a point where the kids waited around specifically to watch my speeches. One of the juniors might get called down to the office, but as soon as I got up in front of the class, he would hang back a bit, just to watch what I was going to say.

Don't misunderstand me – these weren't kids who would pick me up on a Saturday night and take me out partying. But as far as school was concerned, I talked to these kids in the hallways. They would wave at me when they passed by. They *liked* me. I was an alright guy. I was back in the game.

Hey, I was having a really tough time making friends. Not that Jerry was the most loyal buddy a person could ask for, but this happened right when I needed it to, and it helped me out. It was funny, because other freshmen still treated me like I was a shithead. But I got along with the seniors just fine, and it was all because I made them laugh. And laughter goes a long way.

I even mustered up the courage to ask out a senior girl. Alison Maxwell was way, *way* out of my league. When I told one of the other seniors that I was thinking about asking her out, he laughed at me.

"She has a boyfriend," he said, "but if you go through with it, you've got one big, giant set of cohunes."

I *did* ask Alison Maxwell, the hottest girl at our school, out on a date. And she *did* reject me. But you know what? She couldn't have been any nicer about it. I knew what the outcome was going to be. I was fifteen, and I didn't even have my driver's license. What the fuck was I going to do with her? So, there wasn't a lot of disappointment. And even though fifty kids all pointed and laughed at me the next day, I felt like I was on top of the world. I was gaining self-confidence, and that was a completely different kind of experience.

And despite all the assholes and dickheads who laughed at me, there were a few kids who, in my defense, retorted, "Yeah, well, at least *he* had the balls to ask her in the first place."

For a guy who lately felt nothing but loneliness as he sat on a big mountain of shit, life was good.

CHAPTER 7:

Sex, Drugs, and Creative Writing

I was still determined to write the definitive space saga.

In 1997, Lucas re-released the *Star Wars* trilogy to theaters to commemorate the original film's twentieth anniversary. These were the infamous *Special Editions*, and where a lot of fans started to turn their backs on the franchise. But imagine you're a kid in the 90's, who lives, breathes, drinks, and shits *Star Wars*. You've seen the movies on VHS a kazillion times. There are whispers of a prequel trilogy right around the horizon, and this whole new resurgence of the brand – an explosion of video games, comic books, novels, and action figures, all in preparation for the theatrical re-release of these three movies.

And not only that, but Lucas added things. I won't go into detail, but for you fanboys, you know what I'm referring to. I was fascinated at how Lucas was able to take these classic films and breathe new life into them – good *or* bad. Today, with the advent of digital, it's common to see multiple versions of films, and Lucas isn't the only director to dabble into a well-known masterpiece – remember what Spielberg did to "improve" *E.T.*?

New special effects or not, seeing these movies on the big screen for the first time inspired a tidal wave of creativity. That year, I began writing the second *Galactic Redemption* trilogy.

By 1999, I wrote three new books. Originally conceived as prequels to my original trilogy, this new set was more of a reimagining – a term that didn't exist in the late 90's. The new protagonist was Jay Ganthor, who had a lot in common with Jake Houston. However, Jay Ganthor actually had an obstacle – his verbally abusive father, who stopped at nothing to keep Jay on the straight and narrow. That didn't stop Jay from hanging out with a rough, yet fun-loving group of intergalactic rejects, who were threatened by a local bad boy, T Frags. T was doing the bidding of a corrupt general, Bastian Vilkor, who was leading his troops down to Jay's planet in order to gain his footing against overpowering enemy forces. So, all in all, the story had a little more meat to it.

I brought back my duo of space pirates, Garth Gargantuan (my knockoff of Han Solo), and his gargoyle copilot, Jigantus. However, something *Star Wars* hadn't explored (at least back then) was how Han and Chewie first met.

Rather than introducing these characters in the first book, I brought them in to the sequel, *Fall of the Bounty Hunters*, in which Garth and Jigantus meet for the first time before teaming up with Jay Ganthor and his wizard friend, Elkun Hons. In the second book, Jay was pursued by bounty hunters, all sent after him by General Bastian Vilkor. It had an air of *Empire Strikes Back* to it, but there was also a minor villain who trapped the characters colosseum-style. I created a threatening monster called a Zayton, a giant worm that burrowed underground, surfacing in order to eat its prey. It was a nod to that great 90's B-movie classic *Tremors*, but at least I was expanding on my list of inspirations.

By the time I got to the third book, *The Realm of Kinep*, the story eluded me, and I got greedy with the number of characters and locations. At least this time, the planets had variety. There was a droid planet, a lava planet – this pre-dated *Revenge of the Sith* – and even good old Earth served as a location. There were a lot of subplots, and the central narrative got derailed in favor of introducing a slew of new characters. By the time the book ended, it was a colossal mess that concluded with the galaxy being destroyed by a huge black hole. It wasn't the most satisfying conclusion, but at 97 pages, it was the most epic piece of writing I'd ever produced.

At the same time, I was starting another passion project, which I eventually called *Battalion Stealth*. It was another space fantasy, although a self-contained story, and I was writing the whole thing in a loose-leaf notebook.

In my final year of middle school, during graduation, I won the prestigious Writer's Award. My Language Arts teacher presented me with a shiny, silver Cross pen. I had a computer, but I wanted the experience of writing a story longhand.

I spent all four years of high school writing *Battalion Stealth*, and man, was it epic. The main character was an ace pilot and soldier, Retro Knights, who was sent on a top-secret mission. The book began with Retro waking up in the middle of a desert, which, as we find out, was Earth in the future, completely obliterated by the explosion of the sun.

As Earth was constantly bombarded by aggressive alien races, obsessed with scavenging the planet for its leftover resources, the surviving humans established military bases across the planet in the hopes of defending themselves. The backstory involved a heroic woman character, Vera Keetz, who taught the humans how to ward off impending alien invaders. The human race fell into peril when the leader of a major alien threat, General Fanfar of the Cyxloids, came down to Earth and defeated her, kidnapping and imprisoning her inside of his huge, mobile fortress, Neo-5 spaceport.

Then, Vera escaped from her cryo prison fifty years later, only to return to Earth as a stranger, since no one alive remembered who she was.

It was even more epic and messy than *Realm of Kinep*, with each chapter introducing a new alien species, each with their own motives for invading Earth. At one point, all of the human characters split up, and eventually, I completely forgot what the purpose of the story was. It was world building for the sake of world building, but the storyline and the motivations were absent. I was still borrowing elements from movies, but I wasn't grasping why those elements worked. *Battalion Stealth* contained elements of *The Terminator, Independence Day, The Fifth Element* – all of the major sci-fi blockbusters from the 90's. But even though those movies were what people flocked to, they weren't all great movies. *Independence Day*, for example, which was a huge inspiration in writing *Battalion Stealth*, suffers from that exact problem. It has a ton of characters and loads of action, but at the end of the day, what does it all amount to? My writing style and my imagination were there, but I still had no idea how to tell a decent story. And what's more, as much as I wanted to create worlds and write about exotic alien races, I knew next to nothing about the science fiction genre. I hadn't even seen *Star Trek*, at that point. I had very little experience to draw from, and not a lot of rich, sci-fi material to make it all seem believable. When I finished *Battalion Stealth*, it was an accomplishment, but an empty one. It was the last big writing project I embarked on for a while. I needed to find my voice, and I was beginning to wonder if science fiction was really the medium to do that with.

◆ ◆ ◆

In 1999, George Lucas finally released his first *Star Wars* prequel, *Episode I: The Phantom Menace*. This was *the* movie to see that summer. I don't think any movie in the history of cinema received that much hype. I was firing on all cylinders, waiting to see that movie. The trailers looked promising, showcasing the new characters and the types of vehicles we would be introduced to in this new trilogy. We were being re-introduced to familiar characters, albeit younger versions of them. It was a great time to be a *Star Wars* fan.

I loved that movie, and for many years afterwards, I defended the hell out of it. It was just a fun, enjoyable movie. But despite how excited I was, it was not the most influential movie I saw that year.

I had a cousin a few years older than me, who had a driver's license, and so we'd spend a lot of Saturday nights going to the movies. Her dad recommended a movie called *Man on the Moon*, starring Jim Carrey.

Right up front, I wasn't a huge Jim Carrey fan. I liked the *Ace Ventura* films, and *Batman Forever* was alright, but I skipped *The Mask* and *Dumb and Dumber* because I was getting tired of seeing that overly-animated comedic style. I preferred verbal humor over slapstick and gross-out gags, which, as the new century was approaching, was the direction most comedies were taking.

But *Man on the Moon* had my interest because it was rated R, and it wasn't being sold as a straight-up comedy. This was around the time Carrey was doing more dramatic roles, churning out films like *Liar Liar* and *The Truman Show*. And while Andy Kaufman was most notably a comedian, his life story wasn't all laughs.

I had no idea who Andy Kaufman was. I didn't even know the movie was a biopic. The film starts with Jim Carrey explaining, in a weird foreign accent, that the movie we're about to watch is really terrible and therefore, all of the bad parts were removed. He then says that we're actually watching the end of the movie, and before we know it, the credits roll. It turns out to be this big, elaborate joke, and if you were aware of what Kaufman was all about, you probably would have gotten it. But there was something about the type of humor that resonated with me.

In the middle of the film, they started re-enacting scenes from the TV series *Taxi* – and that's when it hit me who this movie was about.

In the late 80's and early 90's, my mom and I stayed up late and watched Nick-at-Nite. Back then, they would air shows from the 50's, 60's, and 70's – shows like *Dick Van Dyke*, *The Marry Tyler Moore Show*, *Mr. Ed*, and occasionally, *Taxi*. I couldn't get into the show, but there was one character I was kind of curious about, and that was the foreign mechanic character, Latka Gravas – played by Andy Kaufman. I remember asking my mom if the actor actually talked like that in real life. He was truly a mystery.

Cut back to *Man on the Moon*, and I realized that Jim Carrey was portraying Andy Kaufman. I was finally getting the joke.

I can't explain how mesmerized I was after watching this movie. I ended up doing a lot of research on Kaufman, even reading his biography. He was fascinating. To say that he was misunderstood would be an understatement.

Kaufman didn't like to be referred to as a comedian, because he didn't want to make a career telling jokes. Truth be told, he hated taping *Taxi*, because that was exactly what he was doing. So, as seen in the film, Kaufman would often tour at colleges and entertain the student body by doing live readings of *The Great Gatsby*; he would go on live television and create uncomfortable situations that often prompted the showrunners to cut to commercial in the middle of a live feed; he would go on the air and insult huge populations of people, then proceed to wrestle women in what was considered one of the low points of his career. Many considered him a practical joker who took the joke too far. He was even voted off of Saturday Night Live during his stint as a Pro Wrestler. It got so bad that when Kaufman passed away from lung cancer, there were tons of people, including his closest friends, who thought he was putting on another act. And that was how the film ended, suggesting that Kaufman faked his death.

Others believed that Kaufman had a behavioral disorder. For all I know, that could have been true. Kaufman would often masquerade as a foul-mouthed, aggressive Vegas lounge singer, Tony Clifton. There was a huge debate about whether Andy and Tony were the same person, even though on all of Clifton's television appearances, he was credited as Tony, not Andy. To further add fuel to the debate, Andy had his best friend and producer, Bob Zmuda (played by Paul Giamatti in the film) make an appearance as Tony Clifton while Andy performed on stage, so that audiences could finally see them onstage together.

There was something undeniably fascinating and appealing to the Andy persona – and I say "persona" because when you listen to interviews from those who knew or worked with Andy, often times they'll say that "there wasn't a real Andy".

Up to this point, I was a good kid, maybe a bit anti-social, who believed in getting the good grades and behaving like a saint. But this idea of celebrating your failures, suffering for your art, even when others fail to see it that way – there was something intriguing about it.

Kaufman was the king of making an audience feel uncomfortable. He marveled at pushing as many buttons as he could, then standing back and laughing at the result – which usually involved audiences booing him off stage, or up and leaving themselves.

As close as I was to graduating high school, I wasn't going to throw that all away. My parents wouldn't have stood for that, and I just didn't have it in me. But when my senior year came around, and I was able to take mostly electives to fill out my graduation requirements, I took as many creative courses as I could. I was going to push the limits of what was acceptable in a high school setting. I was going to explore the barriers of language, creativity, and content. Who was to say what was and wasn't appropriate? I was a rebel – an intellectual and creative rebel, but rebelling all the same.

My speech class was the beginning of that. It didn't happen much, but I started swearing in the middle of my speeches, just to see what kind of reaction I'd get. My classmates applauded my bravery. The teachers – well, how do *you* think they reacted? More times than not, I was told that my material was "inappropriate". Fine. But I was still doing my assignments, I was developing my own creative style, and it was obvious that I didn't phone it in. It was clear that I was putting in the time, and I was developing my language skills even if I was testing the academic waters.

◆ ◆ ◆

Next, I took a drama course. Our first assignment was to stand in front of the class and tell everyone about our backgrounds. I was a clean-cut Jewish kid with a passion for writing. I never tried drugs, not even smoked a cigarette. When I stood in front of the class, I started talking about my history with drugs, my struggle with alcohol – I even dropped a few F-bombs, just to demonstrate that I didn't give a shit about anything.

Did I get any sympathy from my teacher? No. The only feedback I got was that I needed to watch the type of language I used in a high school classroom. It was fucking drama class! To top that off, no one knew that I was making shit up. Wasn't drama about putting on a show? Making your audience believe what you were doing, what you were saying? I guess I was a pretty damn fine actor, because they seemed to buy it.

It didn't help that every performance, every scene I was responsible for crafting, had something to do with getting drunk or getting laid – two things I had never done before. It got to the point where none of my classmates, especially the girls, wanted to work with me because they knew at some point it would involve bed covers and contraceptives. I was just trying to be funny, but no one got that.

At one point, I had to try and play drunk. I wanted to be convincing, so I went around to my classmates, the ones I thought might have some experience with the subject, and asked if they could give me a few pointers. Naturally, the teacher didn't believe me when I told her I had never gotten smashed before. Again, my academy award-winning performance at the beginning of the semester must have really won her over.

It wasn't always about trying to be colorful or offensive. There were times where I'd put some of that aside and tried to be serious about my work. We spent a lot of time practicing the fine art of mime. In one of my acts, I pantomimed the entire sinking of the Titanic. It was an ambitious act, and until the last few moments, the class got what I was trying to do – until the ship sank, and then I looked like a beach whale doing aquatic porno.

My favorite bit was the bobsled. There were four of us in a group, and we took four chairs, lining them up single-file to represent a bobsled. During our act, we moved the chairs back and forth in unison, simulating the start of our epic bobsled run. One by one, we each leapt into our respective chairs, and then we went through the motions, like we were whipping around corners. Then, I stood up in my chair to check out what was going on, and I got decapitated. I tucked my head into my shirt and slumped over in my seat. The guy behind me, Trevor, acted as if he caught my head in mid-air, and then started juggling my head in his hands. Then, all of us started going out of control. The bit ended with us all crashing, falling out of our now-tipped over chairs. It actually got a few laughs from the teacher.

◆ ◆ ◆

But where I *really* started testing the waters was in creative writing. It was tough, because the teacher was a strict Catholic with no tolerance for swearing in her classroom. So, what happened when I started swearing like a truck driver in my creative pieces?

It turned out that she was okay with a little "colorful language" as long as it enhanced the story. But she knew what I was doing was purely for shock value, and so did my classmates. And she wasn't happy with it. One, she knew I had potential as a writer. Why was I wasting my talent on such garbage? She wanted me to write literature, and I was giving her cheap, dime-store pulp stories.

I should stop here and mention that this was when I discovered the movie *Clerks*. If you've gotten this far, my love of

Kevin Smith films shouldn't be a shock to you. But for those of you who picked up this book simply because the cover looked interesting:

Clerks is a black-and-white indie film written and directed by Kevin Smith, a New Jersey-based filmmaker who would go on to have a long film and acting career; the dude also has strong ties in the comic book community.

But back when he was starting out, Kevin Smith was just a small-time aspiring filmmaker who dropped out of film school, maxed out a bunch of credit cards, and hired a bunch of his friends to make a movie that cost $27,000. On the surface, *Clerks* is exactly what it sounds like: two smart-ass convenience store clerks sit around all day as they tear apart pop-culture, rip apart customers, and become insubordinate in order to fulfill personal obligations.

This was at a time when I was expanding my moviegoing options. I frequented local video stores, renting movies that I'd heard about, but never took the time to watch. And obviously, if you've seen *Clerks*, then you know what scene really stood out to me.

While *Clerks* is heavy in dialogue, if you take the time to analyze it, the conversations between Dante and Randal are profoundly clever. They don't just sit around and talk about movies – that's what happens when amateur filmmakers try to *imitate* Kevin Smith – but they over-analyze the simplest things.

Case in point: Randal and Dante's discussion regarding *Return of the Jedi*. First off, I was blown away that I was watching a movie in which two characters were discussing *Star Wars* at such great lengths. I never saw a movie where characters literally sat around for five minutes and talked about the "holy trilogy". That blew my mind. Not only do they discuss the trilogy, but the music playing during the conversation is a song called "Chewbacca", performed by a band called Supernova. But it wasn't until my second or third time watching that scene that I realized the true genius of Smith's writing.

In the scene, Randal specifically talks about the second

Death Star, and how, when the Rebels blew it up, it was still under construction. If you've seen *Return of the Jedi*, you already know that. But what's bothering Randall is that, because the Death Star was incomplete, there were still innocent independent contractors onboard who were blown up as a result of its destruction. Think about that for a second. It's a well-known science fiction movie, complete with lasers, lightsabers, and Ewoks, and for the first time, the moral choices of the Rebel Alliance are brought into question thanks to the possibility of innocent construction workers being blown up due to their ignorance revolving around personal politics. Mind. Blown.

The film is full of those types of analytic conversations, and few people can whip around dialogue like Kevin Smith.

At the time I saw *Clerks*, the film was part of what Smith called his New Jersey trilogy, which was also comprised of *Mallrats* and *Chasing Amy*. The three films are not directly related, but rather exist in the same universe; characters from one film might reference something that happened in another. While *Mallrats* didn't leave much of an impression (I *do* love the scene with Stan Lee, though), *Chasing Amy* hit close to home.

Chasing Amy was a jumping-off vehicle for Ben Affleck, who was largely unknown back then. The film is about a New Jersey-based comic book artist who falls in love with a hip Jersey girl – only to find out she's a lesbian. Again, it employs a lot of Smith's sharp, poignant dialogue, and delves into the complexity of relationships. This was a film that I tried to constantly emulate when I eventually shifted gears and headed into filmmaking.

But for the time, it inspired me to write a play called *Leon's Tragedy*.

I was impressionable, even at seventeen. If I saw a style I liked, I tried to copy it. One of the earlier pieces I did for the creative writing class was a short subject called *Short Future*. It was puzzling to those who read it because, as an aspiring science fiction writer, I was telling a coming-of-age story that was set in the future. Just think of *Catcher in the Rye* with a science fiction twist, and not as iconic.

Short Future told the story of a high school teenager, Leon – essentially, he was me. Anyone outside of Berkley High School wouldn't have understood it, because a big part of it was reacting to the changes taking place that year and exaggerating them. But it was also about a kid desperately trying to fit in, and not being able to find his place. Sound familiar? Yeah, seems to be a running theme in this book. It also dealt with another frustration – striking out with girls. It made a lot of my classmates uncomfortable, because they knew I struggled with these things.

Leon was a character who kept popping up in my short stories – hence, creating a "shared universe" like that of Kevin Smith. Other students eventually included Leon in *their* stories, as a nod to what I was doing, so hey, I was on to something.

Coming back to *Leon's Tragedy*: first of all, this was supposed to be a one-act play. If you've been paying attention, you know I watch movies, not stage plays. I had no idea how a play was structured. So, my one-act play had seventeen acts, complete with scene changes and the type of transitions common in film. The story was a personal one. I drew from the whole "Jessie & Jerry" fiasco, and I used *Chasing Amy* as a template.

I was at that age when it's almost impossible to look at things subjectively. Looking back at that whole experience, I know I wasn't a perfect friend. I'll even go a step further and admit that I pushed my friends away. But it took a long time for me to get to that point, and for years, I painted myself as the victim. *Leon's Tragedy* became a very one-sided argument, and guess who came out smelling like roses?

I made Jessie and Jerry look like a couple of shitheads. It contained material I had no business talking about, like making Jerry a pothead. It was a two-dimensional, borderline cartoonish portrayal. When Jerry and I were still friends, Jerry wasn't even a smoker. When everything came to an end, I knew Jerry turned to drugs, and I'm pretty sure I saw him when he was high once, but you would have thought the guy was a bona fide heroin junkie after reading my play.

Aside from the subject matter, which not only discussed relationships, but also involved explicit sexual content, there was the language. Everyone knew I was taking a page from the Kevin Smith bible, and it was just another thing that made the classroom uncomfortable. I think deep down, my classmates applauded my boldness. But they also knew how conservative our teacher was, and they knew I was trying to push her buttons, trying to see how far I could take it without getting into trouble.

I was at constant odds with our teacher. I understand, looking back, that there are certain things you just can't say in a high school classroom. But I also wasn't swearing at my teachers, or acting out. I was expressing myself creatively, and that's something I've always felt should be encouraged.

Society is always talking about the negative effects of bullying, and how to prevent it from happening. It's all bullshit. But your basic, textbook bully is someone looking for a way to vent their frustrations, and usually it manifests itself through violence. Think what kind of a world it would be if more bullies, rather than stabbing their mother in the jugular or killing twenty of their classmates, wrote a play about a kid who just got the best blowjob ever? Hell, even *writing* about a kid shooting up his school is better than *doing* that same thing. Wouldn't you agree?

The best part of *Leon's Tragedy* was getting to read it out loud in front of the class. It was hysterical, because some of the students had fun with it and read whatever was on the page. Then there were others who censored themselves for fear of what our teacher might say. Yes, I *did* write it for shock value, but I also had a personal story to tell. I was putting myself out there for everyone to see, and asking them, "What do you think about this?" Some people sympathized with Leon, understanding where he was coming from, and others hated the character and thought he had no redeemable qualities. It generated a lot of discussion, it was considered risqué and, god forbid, maybe even controversial (remember, this *was* a high school piece).

And despite the teacher questioning it, even she couldn't deny that at least the kids were talking about it. It was fun to stir up some shit, creatively speaking.

And just to prove to our creative writing teacher that I could write something that was above pure shock value, I wrote a piece called *The Tony Clifton Story*, inspired by the one-and- only Andy Kaufman. To give some additional context, back in the late 70's / early 80's, Kaufman and his writing partner Bob Zmuda were trying to launch Andy's film career. Together, they wrote *The Tony Clifton Story*, which would have been a biopic about Andy's infamous alter ego. Universal optioned the film, but when Andy starred in a romantic comedy called *Heartbeeps,* the movie flopped and Universal quickly shelved *Tony Clifton.*

Using Kaufman's supposed "faking his death" angle, my story took place in the present day, and the narrator witnessed a Tony Clifton performance at the Comedy Store. The narrator thinks it's Bob Zmuda giving the performance, when he finds out at the end that it's Andy all along. The story captured some of Andy's most memorable performances, such as his spot-on Elvis Presley impersonation, but it also captured some great Tony Clifton-isms. The teacher loved it, saying it was one of the best things she read all year long. Talk about a complete one-eighty.

CHAPTER 8:

My Three Shitty High School Films

Remember that interview between Leonard Maltin and George Lucas? That was the first time I thought about making movies for a living. I remembered thinking that you had to be rich, or well-connected, to make movies.

But *Clerks* was the film where I said, "Maybe I *can* do this."

I grew up watching blockbusters, and you probably couldn't make *Independence Day* on the cheap. It wasn't until my senior year that I started to explore the world of indie cinema.

With today's technology, anyone can make a movie. Anybody. But in the early 2000's, cell phones were still primitive, high definition was a few years off, and camcorders were big and bulky. Even the smaller digital camcorders, which recorded on mini cassettes, were bulkier than what's available today. Non-linear editing software, like Adobe Premiere and Avid, were luxuries that aspiring filmmakers couldn't afford.

My newfound interest in filmmaking led me to take my first video production course. This was the class responsible for producing those obnoxious morning announcements that were broadcast to every classroom, if your school was fortunate enough to have such a thing. The course was geared more toward ENG – Electronic News Gathering – than on filmmaking, but I was able to get my feet wet with some of the equipment, specifically with the editing bays. This was before the convenience of SD cards, where you had to digitize your footage into the computer before working with it. It was the first time I was able to grasp what really went on behind the scenes. It was basic stuff, but I was able to generate titles and include music tracks.

The only downside: whatever I worked on had to be related to class. If I was going to take on the daunting task of making my own movies, the school's equipment was off-limits.

This is where it really pays to be creative. You want to know how I made my first film, with no editing equipment? There's nothing like a good word processor and a pair of VCRs.

The first film I ever made was an adaptation of my short story, *Short Future*. I chose it for one basic reason: the setting. *Short Future* was set in high school. The first rule for indie filmmakers with no money: use what's available.

The idea was that I would act and direct, shooting most of the footage in between classes. I would attempt to shoot the last scene, which took place in a classroom, during my creative writing class. That part was tricky, because I had a limited amount of time, and that was only if the teacher allowed it.

Luckily, my classmates didn't mind. They saw it as an excuse to get out of doing classwork. The teacher was fine with the idea, provided it didn't cut into her learning plan. This meant that I would have to shoot the last scene over several days, and I knew that no one would come to class wearing the same clothes from the day before. It was an editor's worst nightmare.

I used my dad's old 8mm camcorder, which hadn't seen the light of day since my bar mitzvah five years prior. It was primal, and unlike the modern models, it didn't have an LCD screen. If I wanted to check my footage, I had to rely on the black-and-white viewfinder, or connect it to a VCR. If I was on-location, I would have no idea what my audio sounded like, because it didn't have speakers. And if you're asking, "Why didn't you monitor your audio with headphones?" Yeah, the camera didn't have a headphone jack, either. I might as well have been capturing video with a stone tablet and a chisel.

The camera had an option to place black bars on the top and bottom edges of the screen, to give the impression of a more cinematic look. The only reason I chose this option was because DVDs were becoming more prevalent, and audiences were starting to get used to watching movies this way. But because I had no idea how to properly frame a shot, the effect didn't pan out. All throughout production, the tops of peoples' heads got chopped off. It looked like the person behind the camera had no idea what they were doing. And I didn't.

To make matters worse, I had no script. I used my own source material as a reference and fudged it as I went. Because I was in such a rush to get it finished, and self-conscious about running around with a video camera, I didn't have time to memorize lines. This meant that in the middle of a shot, I looked down at my short story to see what dialogue came next. That's why, if you head over to YouTube to watch this travesty of a film, you'll notice that the camera tilts down drastically during most of the shots.

Once I had all the footage, I decided I needed titles. I came up with an incredibly amateur method: using Microsoft Word, I typed all the text against a black background, and pointed the camera at the monitor as I sat off to the side, scrolling the text with my mouse. It served its purpose, but it also had a number of issues. When you point a camera at a television screen, you almost never get a clear picture. Usually, you'll see a bunch of wavy lines intruding on the image. Secondly, without a tripod, I had to use other means to keep the camera steady, like a stack of books. This meant that the image was usually crooked, and oftentimes you could see the borders of the monitor. Third, the camera had no manual focus option, so at such a high contrast level, the camera auto-focused between the edges of the monitor and the super-bright text on the screen. So, a lot of the text was barely legible.

Because the story of *Short Future* was set in the future, the idea was that the school was located in the sky, like Hill Valley in *Back to the Future Part II*, and people drove flying cars. I was an avid Howard Stern listener in those days, so in the story, Leon drove to school listening to Howard Stern IV. That explains why I'm listening to Howard Stern in the film.

And obviously, I couldn't use special effects given my limited film background, so how did I accomplish the feat of filming a flying car? I stole footage from *Back to the Future Part II*.

I was once again testing the waters, splicing in footage that I knew would get me in trouble. As risqué as some of it was, I could have gone much further. I never completely broke the rules, but for one specific scene, I got dangerously close to crossing that threshold.

In the middle of the film, I'm sitting in the cafeteria, talking to my best friend, Neil Jefferson. Neil had been my new BFF since sophomore year, and was helping me film a lot of the movie. In the scene, I was supposed to have a crush on a really attractive girl, and in the story, Leon hits on her, getting rejected. The problem was, I couldn't find anyone who wanted to play my love interest, even after I explained to them that it was only "acting". So, I looked off-camera, as if I were checking out this girl, and then I cut to footage from *Private Parts*, the feature film about Howard Stern. Which scene did I splice in, you might ask? The scene where Howard's at the airport, fantasizing about the scantily-dressed woman, imagining her breasts growing to cartoonish proportions.

It got a laugh from the class, probably because it was so unexpected, and it was such a jarring edit. The teacher hated it and threatened to turn the video off in the middle of the class viewing if it continued to go into that territory.

Short Future was fun to make, and it's still fun to laugh at for nostalgia sakes, but for the casual viewer, it's nearly unbearable to watch. The story gets lost (even the original source material isn't too engrossing), and most of it looks like some goofy high school video that some idiot shot in between classes because he had too much spare time. But the criticisms about the shaky camera movement and lack of storytelling *did* help when I pursued later productions.

◆ ◆ ◆

In the summer of 1999, leading up to the release of *Episode I*, I discovered that a lot of aspiring filmmakers produced their own *Star Wars* fan films. They were plastered all over the internet. Even before the advent of YouTube, there were entire databases dedicated to fan-made *Star Wars* films. Some of them were extremely ambitious. A few kids had gotten hold of special effects software and crafted their own lightsabers, and they looked pretty damn good, about as good as anything you'd see in the real movies! One crew did *Macbeth*, complete with iambic pentameter, and they brought in elements from *Star Wars*, where Macbeth was Darth Vader! There were some truly epic lightsaber fights, and even some stuff with stop-motion animation and action figures. Even the films that were complete technical garbage were entertaining. I spent hours after school downloading fan-films and getting inspired.

In video production class, I met fellow moviegoer, Dan. At first, I didn't think I'd click with him. He was two grades behind me, and he hung around with some real winners (sarcasm). That year, to pass the time, I watched movies on my dad's new portable DVD player. This caught Dan's interest, and we suddenly started talking about movies. He introduced me to George Romero's *Dead* trilogy, and I shared my passion of Jason and Freddy movies. We teamed up together on a lot of in-class video assignments.

Dan had outgrown *Star Wars*, and that year, he gave me his entire Micro Machines collection – that included a Stormtrooper playset and a ton of thumbnail-sized figurines. The playset resembled a Stormtrooper on the outside, but when you opened it up, it became the inside of the Death Star, complete with a miniature trash compactor. This became the main set piece for my next film.

When Jerry Breckinfield and I were still chums, we sat

around discussing possibilities for a *Star Wars* porn parody. Today, a ton of these things exist, most of them baring the most obvious title: *Star Whores.* But before that took off, and before Kevin Smith came up with the title for *his* movie, *Zack and Miri Make a Porno*, we had our own version. What would the characters be called? Jabba the Slut. Princess I'm-a-Dollar. Emperor Puff-My-Dick. Solo Hand. Princess I-Wanna-Lay-Her. You could do this all day long. Want a fun drinking game? Take a shot every time you come up with a *Star Wars* porno name.

The proposed title for my next magnum opus was *Star Wars: Episode XXX – The Phantom Condom.* The funny thing is, the title was purely an attention getter. With the exception of a few characters shouting out raunchy names for the starships (like Ass Fighters, Pussy Fighters, and Clitorous Fighters – I guess Imperial TIE Fuckers and ASS-ASS Walkers were already taken), there is absolutely no sex to be had in my film. Not one character is seen fornicating. Not even C-3PO. Talk about false advertising.

The whole movie took place in my bedroom. There was no set dressing, here. In every frame, you can see my posters, my computer monitor, and my VHS collection. You can even spot Tony Clifton on my desktop's background. I shot it in the winter time, so I brought in lumps of snow from my front yard to serve for the ice planet Hoth.

There were some exhilarating dogfights, where I wrapped the end of a wire coat hanger around the rear end of an X-Wing and literally hung it in front of the camera, emulating Lucas's sophisticated method of putting large, detailed models on wires back in the 70's. But if I'm being completely honest (and when am I not?), half the film looks like my camera is spinning in a complete circle around my room, and it makes for nauseating viewing.

Another problem was capturing action figures as small as my thumbnail. Remember, these were Micro Machines, which meant the camera auto-focused between the action figures and my fingers. It makes the whole experience that much more irritating.

With no editing software at my disposal, I had to figure out how to get creative with titles, so I used the same technique of recording yellow text against a black background. I also wanted this movie to *sound* like a *Star Wars* film. I played John Williams' epic score in the background, on my stereo, while recording the footage. This made for a HUGE problem later on, because unless I re-recorded all the voices, I was stuck with the music in every shot. It was married to my footage. To make it even more horrible, I didn't bother to hide my stereo *or* my music collection. In certain shots, you get a perfect view of my CD binders *and* my big-ass boombox just chilling on my bed, a part of the scenery.

Then there were my parents. By this time, they were at the tail-end of their marriage, and their relationship deteriorated from merely shitty to full-on diarrhea. My mom would come home from work and start yelling at my dad, and they would argue for hours on end. Even with my door closed, you could hear them fighting in the next room. If you listen closely, you can hear my mom carrying on in the background. It's uncomfortable, and in later years, upon revisiting the film, I tried to mask their arguing with some *Star Wars* sound effects. In the raw footage, it's hard to ignore.

The movie starts with an opening logo: Lennieth Century Fox. I thought it was cute. Then, those familiar blue words show up on the screen:

A long time ago in a bedroom far, far away...

Then we have the opening crawl:

"Those Imperial sons of bitches have once again screwed it all up for the Rebel Bastards. Little do they know that the sinister Darth Vader, somehow resurrected, has gained a big, red erection in all of this.

The bastard Rebels, who can't get anymore retarded, struggle to find the planet Hoth, where they are met with a retarded, sucky surprise attack. Damn.

With a small supply of douche bags and an annoying goldenrod at their side, the band of retards make their way across the cold reaches of space in hopes of once again conquering Vader and destroying his incredible new weapon...."

Speechless? A lot of kids were when I showed them the finished film during lunch period. They had a fun time watching it, but only because it was so dreadfully bad. The teacher whose classroom we used said it looked like the cameraman was drunk. Yeah, it did. But you can judge for yourselves: the full 35-minute (!) film is available on YouTube.

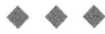

My next film would also serve as a class project, and even though I'd be testing the waters once again, I really wanted this one to show an improvement over *Short Future*. This was a simple task: just keep my ass away from the camera.

The film would be based on Sophocles' Athenian tragedy, *Oedipus Rex*. This was perfect. There was nothing I could put in this movie that could be more perverse than a son having incestual relations with his mother. I could do anything I wanted, as long as it was relevant to the source material.

And that's what got me in trouble.

Oedipus the King was the first time I went through the trouble of writing a script. I also wanted to challenge myself with the locations, not limiting myself to school hallways or my bedroom (although there would be certain things happening *within* the bedroom, if you catch my drift, wink, wink).

My Language Arts teacher was a funny, sophisticated African American woman named Mrs. Reynolds. Language Arts was always a class I excelled in, so I tended to opt for the advanced placement courses, even if some of my other teachers thought the medium-level classes better suited me. While I was adept at writing essays, I had a short attention span when it came to literature. "But how can this be when you're writing a book?"

I'm glad you asked.

Literature bores the ever-living piss out of me, plain and simple. The only reason we read such classics as *Catcher in the Rye, Wuthering Heights, Animal Farm, 1984*, and *The Fountainhead* is so we can analyze symbolism, discuss hidden meanings, and study character development. That's fine and dandy, but the kinds of books I enjoyed reading had everything spelled out on the page. And the worst thing about reading as coursework is that, the teacher doesn't allow you to reach your own conclusions: they expect you to arrive at *their* conclusions. There really is no critical thinking involved. Take notes based on what the *teacher* got out of the reading, and pass the test.

Mrs. Reynolds followed the basic formula, but she gave us a little more leeway to argue other points, as long as we properly supported our argument. You still had to hit all of her bullet points for the exam, but she allowed discussions to go off on other tangents. She was also supportive of creativity. I showed her some rough sketches I did while writing my magnum opus, *Battalion Stealth*, and she was amazed at how much energy I put into a piece that wasn't school-related.

Like my creative writing teacher, Mrs. Reynolds was also highly conservative. And keep in mind, this was an advanced placement course, where all the really smart, academic students enrolled. Intellectually, I was at their level, but behaviorally, I don't think they were ready for what I had in store.

Earlier that semester, we read George Orwell's *1984*, a futuristic dystopian novel in which an entire society is under the constant watch of Big Brother – a commentary on our government. For my student project, I made an audio cassette tape, essentially a skit, where I "interviewed" characters from the book, like a radio broadcast, complete with music and sound effects. Parts of it were legit, but then there were parts that went completely off the rails. I made inappropriate comments about some of the teachers, and I even got Neil in on the act. He used this guttural British accent, and he went off the cuff. It was funny, but a lot of it wasn't relevant to the source material. I was trying to amuse myself but failed at serving the project requirements. Mrs. Reynolds didn't know what to make of it, and halfway through its playthrough, she cut it off in front of the class and told me she couldn't grade it because it was too offensive. I was never so embarrassed. Even my classmates had no idea what to make of it. Was I trying to be the class clown? Was I just craving attention? Was I high?

I was just trying to get a laugh.

With *Oedipus the King*, I was dead set on maintaining the integrity of Sophocles' play. But the process of screen adaptation is a funny thing. Rarely are the book and the movie one and the same. The assignment was to create a video that touched on the themes of the play, but set in a modern setting. What if we saw Oedipus and his wife/mother, Jocasta, in bed together? Taboo? Sure. But the whole story is a taboo. Sigmund Freud's concept of the Oedipus complex came from this very play. So, why would there be anything wrong with showing an intimate bedroom scene between two of the central characters?

Because it was high school. It didn't make any sense to me. We could *read* this filth, but we couldn't *watch* it? And let's face it, it might be hard to ignore the play's historical significance, but this was the *Game of Thrones* of its day.

I had two classmates help me with the project, Megan Dorny and Ivan Panovich. Neither one wanted to write an essay, but as long as they shared a fair amount of screen time in the video, they'd get credit for it. Megan was going to play Jocasta, my love interest, who I later find out is my biological mother. Ivan played the prophet Tiresias, as well as Oedipus's royal servant (a character I completely made up) and one of his sons. I even got Dan to act in the film, playing Oedipus's other son, as well as his brother-in-law, Creon. Dan would also have a minor, yet crucial, role – one that dictated the outcome of the whole project.

The first scene took place in my bedroom. The opening shot lingers on a ceiling fan, and then tilts down to Megan and me lying in bed. The song "True Companion" is playing in the background, a bit I picked up from the film *Heavy Metal,* which I was a huge fan of. We've just performed "the act" – even though both of us are fully clothed – and Megan is pretending to smoke a cigarette as we talk openly about our sex life.

"Oh, Ody – it's never been like that before," Megan says.

"Yeah, I get like that sometimes," I respond, feigning a huge erection beneath the covers, which I faked using a ruler. It was stupid, goofy shit like that, and according to Mrs. Reynolds, completely out of line. But we weren't simulating sex. We weren't doing anything inappropriate, aside from sitting in bed and having an intimate conversation about something that happened off-screen. I was trying to demonstrate that if *Oedipus Rex* was adapted today, the sexuality would be at the forefront, and not just subtext created by some perverted playwright with mommy issues.

As the scene plays on, Oedipus's surfer-lingo-spouting servant clues him in to his possible heritage, and that's when Oedipus seeks out Tiresias, the blind prophet in the know.

Here's the thing: I decided to make the prophet a porn addict. I liked this idea ever since I saw the Mel Brooks film *Robin Hood: Men in Tights.* There's a blind character named Blinkin who, upon being introduced, is reading an issue of *Playboy* – and it's in braille. He's *feeling up* the centerfold. I loved that concept, and honestly, I just wanted to get a laugh. And it was still relevant to the story, because Tiresias was a character from the source material who served as the exposition.

The second act of the film, which is Oedipus's big revelation scene, was shot at Shepherd Park, across the street from where I lived as a boy. It was supposed to double for the land of Thebes, where the story is set. The scene starts with this panoramic shot of the park. It's hilarious, because it was basically a big playground, complete with swing sets, a life-sized wooden train that kids could climb on, and a colored stack of tires. At the edge of the park was a wooded area, but the playground stuck out like a sore thumb because of all the vibrant colors.

You can plainly see cars driving in the background, but in a sense, this helped because I was supposed to be adapting the story for a contemporary setting.

Shooting at this place was a nightmare. For one, it was logistically hard to get all four of us to the park at the same time. We all had different extracurricular activities. Megan had band, Ivan was an athlete, and Dan had no real obligation to be there because it wasn't his class.

Like with *Short Future,* I shot the scene over two days – the first day with Ivan, and the second with Megan, which is why in the film, you never see them in the same shot.

Because I had my driver's license, I had to take my youngest brother, Glenn, with me wherever I went. Trying to look after a six-year-old while you're trying to film a movie is virtual torture. I couldn't keep Glenn from running into every shot. He had an entire playground at his disposal. This was in the evening, an hour before sunset. The park was empty. And what he wanted to do was run around beating garbage cans with a stick. It was a good thing my shitty-ass camcorder picked up every background sound.

Then there was Ivan's "illness". When I went to pick him up, he just ate a chili dog, so halfway to the park, he screamed at me repeatedly to pull over. I pulled over, he jumped out, and he yacked just mere inches from my car. I thought I was going to have to take him back home and try again at some point during the week. This wasn't exactly a leisure pursuit. It was a class assignment, which meant I had a tight deadline.

Thankfully, Ivan felt great after emptying his guts, and we were able to film the scene. We got to the top of this hill, which overlooked the entire park. I had my boombox with me, so I could play music while recording the scene. The selection was John Powell's score for the movie *Face/Off*, an excellent John Woo flick with John Travolta and Nicolas Cage.

My camera had no LCD screen, so I couldn't check my audio levels. I had to trust that the dialogue was being recorded cleanly. I was leaving most of the camerawork up to Dan, since he was barely in this scene. I gave him basic camera directions, like rotating 360 degrees around us for one shot – pretty ambitious, given the little cinematic knowledge I had. It was filmed against a sunset, so it was the most visually striking thing I'd shot.

In the scene, I confront Ivan, as Tiresias, and the first thing we see is that he's holding out a centerfold for what is clearly a *Playboy* magazine, which I grabbed from my dad's stash. It was right out of that scene from *Men in Tights*. I made sure this was a wide-shot, so anyone watching really wouldn't see much. But the exchange of dialogue was what got me in trouble:

Oedipus: You there! Shepherd!
Tiresias: (Holding the Playboy*) Coming, Mom!*
Oedipus: (Grabs the magazine) What is this? This filth? You're reading porno, in my land? My lovely land of Thebes? You, of all... Porn, what is this?
(Oedipus and Tiresias fold out the centerfold, both staring at the pictures.)
Tiresias: This was on page 46!
Oedipus: Well, that's odd. Maybe me and Jocasta should try this thing on page 46!

Yes, the scene gets a bit sidetracked. I added an unflattering personal trait in an attempt to get a laugh. But Mrs. Reynolds was appalled. As my classmates watched it, there was this uneasy silence in the room. You could hear a pin drop, even with the video running.

It's the next shot that killed the project for me.

While we filmed the scene, I grabbed the magazine and tossed it to the ground. Then the explanation for Oedipus's heritage came into play. But Dan, a guy who had the same sense of humor as me, came up with a brilliant idea that had me in stitches. Right after I tossed the magazine to the ground, I shot a close-up of the magazine. Then Dan randomly stepped into the shot, picked up the mag from the ground, and shouted, "Yes! Porno!" He then proceeded to walk off-camera with the magazine, this shit-eating grin on his face. To Dan, Ivan, and me, it was a moment of comic brilliance.

I went home that night and started watching the footage, hooking the camcorder up to my trusty CRT TV. The stuff with the *Playboy* cracked me up, no doubt about it. This was some grade A, quality funny shit.

Then the expositional part came on, where I was beating Ivan to the ground, forcing him to tell me who I really was. This was the scene where I had the music playing in the background.

The dialogue was barely audible. The music was too overpowering. And because it was a part of the soundtrack, there was no way to replace it without reshooting the entire scene. I was heart-broken. All these years later, even with everything that's available, I've never found a way to fix that scene. Looking back, I could have kicked myself. I should have recorded the scene without the music, and during the playback in class, I could have had a music CD playing on the side, to give the impression that our film had music. I didn't realize that years later, I'd actually have access to editing software where I'd be able to edit it back into the film.

But I didn't have time to reshoot. We had a week to record everything. So, I left it as it was recorded, and just hoped to God the class would be able to understand what we were saying in the scene.

Of course, I had to incorporate some *Star Wars* references. The next day, when Megan came down to the park to shoot her scene, I had her wear a flimsy Darth Vader mask. This was the crucial scene where Jocasta was going to reveal her true relationship to Oedipus. In true George Lucas fashion, she slides on the mask and utters, "Ody... I am your mother." Comic gold? No. But I remembered that awesome production of *Macbeth*, and I really wanted to emulate that. *Oedipus* was nowhere near that level of production, but I tried. I really, *really* tried.

In the play, once *Oedipus* realizes what he's done, Jocasta commits suicide by hanging herself, and Oedipus stabs out his eyes, symbolic of how this whole time, he's been blind to his past.

I was not a make-up artist. I had no idea how I was going to simulate that scene. But I was creative.

I set the final act on Halloween. Oedipus, deranged after finding out all this information, enters the scene wearing a hockey mask – his costume for Halloween – and prepares to get his kids ready for trick-or-treating, when he stumbles into his bedroom and sees Jocasta at the end of a rope.

To film this scene, I used a Darth Vader figurine, and tied him to one of the blades of my ceiling fan. I loved this, because not only was it humorous, but it made my opening shot – the shot of the ceiling fan – feel symbolic. I was quite proud of myself for that one. Here I was, an amateur filmmaker, thinking cinematically for a change.

I had Ivan wear a black glove, and I shot a close-up of his hand, as if he was now Jocasta in the Vader costume. Oedipus finds his beloved mother holding a knife, and using it, he stabs out his eyes. I wore the hockey mask, so I was able to stick the blade of the prop knife through each of the eye holes, screaming bloody murder. It was great, if I do say so myself. You would have thought I was in real, physical pain.

It took me several tries to get the knife to go through the eye hole at the right angle. The blade was rubber, and it kept bending every time I couldn't get it to go in at the proper angle. Ivan laughed his ass off behind the camera. At one point, he asked, "Can't you just cut to it already in there?"

Then there was the final scene, the "Epilogue", where Oedipus is rejected from the world by his kids (who retaliate by calling him a loser and giving him the finger), and his brother-in-law, Creon. In the final shot, Creon banishes Oedipus from Thebes, when his daughter, Antigone, offers to aid him in his exile. The last line in the film has me proclaiming, "Great Scott!" as I fall flat to the ground. You can guess what movie reference I stole that from. And the film ends, incidentally, with Alan Silvestri's classic *Back to the Future* score, and the words "To be continued..." popping up on the screen.

When I showed the finished film to Megan and Ivan, we had a blast. Even though it was technically inferior, we had a lot of fun making it, and the result was fifteen minutes of hilarious entertainment. We thought we struck gold. Mrs. Reynolds would get our jokes, she would understand all my attempts at cinematic symbolism, and we'd all go home smiling with our A's.

What really happened was Mrs. Reynolds watched the film right up to Dan's infamous "Yes, porno!" scene, walked to the front of the class, turned off the tape, and handed it back to me. "If you want to watch this garbage, do it on your own time. This is offensive to me and everyone else in here. Come see me after class so we can discuss a suitable assignment. I'm not grading this."

She said this in front of everyone. There I stood, in a classroom full of honor students – and I include myself in that group – and no one understood what I was doing. They looked at me like I should have known better. I wonder what made those kids laugh, because apparently, a little toilet humor wasn't for them.

And that's all it was! *South Park* was in its first or second season, and everyone in school talked about it – even people in my Language Arts class! But a little poke at sexuality, when the source material had this huge plot point centered around incest, and that was taking things too far.

I felt worse for Ivan and Megan, because their grades were riding on this. The three of us now had to write essays, which was what we wanted to avoid in the first place. I didn't have any extracurricular activities to worry about, but they didn't have time to do a lengthy research paper on a guy with severe mother issues.

I wasn't going to take this lying down. What got me going was, she refused to watch the rest of the video. She stopped it based on an irrelevant scene that had nothing to do with the rest of our film. There was an entire third act she wouldn't attempt to watch because the idea of Ivan and me holding that *Playboy* was too upsetting.

I defended my choices, but at that point, Mrs. Reynolds made her decision. To her, I failed to meet the requirements of the assignment. She learned that with me, there was a pattern. After the *1984* tape, I couldn't be trusted to use any other kind of media aside from print. And she didn't like my essays because they were too long.

Yeah, that was a running theme with me. I liked to write. And I had a hard time sticking to a small page requirement. If I was asked to write three pages, I'd write ten. It wasn't because I was trying to be facetious; I just had a lot to say on any given subject.

One time, I turned in a twenty-five paged fantasy story – but the page limit was five. Mrs. Reynolds wouldn't look at it. She handed it back and challenged me to condense it to five pages. After I spent the time revising it, she didn't understand the story because I cut too much out. The only way she agreed to give me a fair grade was if I resubmitted the original piece so she could make sense of it all, which I did. I got an A, but I really had to work for that one.

Regarding *Oedipus*, I felt she was being unreasonable. If she agreed to watch the video from beginning to end, and she felt that we didn't meet the requirements, I could have lived with that. But to get bent out of shape over a stupid sex joke, so much so that she refused to grade us, was not fair.

I didn't know what else to do, so I talked about it with my dad. He knew how hard I worked on it. He made a call to the school and talked to the principal. The next day, I anxiously asked Mrs. Reynolds if she watched the rest of the tape.

She still couldn't get past the infamous "Yes, porno" line. I explained that the line was a throw-away joke and admitted it didn't have any relevance to the plot of *Oedipus*. So, I offered to take the line out, just so she could get past this horrible segment and give us a fucking grade, already. But she had enough. She didn't want to watch the rest, because she was already too repulsed by everything that came before – and the *1984* episode didn't help my case.

I went home that night and prepared my essay, writing out my thesis statement and outlining the body, like I'd been taught since junior high. It might have been the first time I wasn't passionate about a writing assignment. Imagine working so hard on something, and then having to do it all over again. The second time through, it doesn't come out as well, because you spent all your energy on that first time, creating something. No matter what paper I was going to write, it wasn't going to be an A paper because frankly, my dear, I didn't give a damn.

I walked in the next day, ready to present the topic of my paper to Mrs. Reynolds. She handed Megan, Ivan, and me a B+ on the film. Apparently, she fast-forwarded through the offensive one-liner that was driving her bat-shit crazy, and she was able to watch the rest of the film. And wouldn't you know it? She found it – are you ready for this? – quite funny. She liked the shot with Darth Vader hanging from the ceiling fan, the scene where I gouge out my eyes, and the epilogue, complete with Ivan and Dan flicking me off and calling me a loser as Creon banishes my incestuous, newly-blinded ass from Thebes.

I've painted this picture of a prudish, unfair teacher intent on making me work overtime just to get a grade. I never saw her as a horrible person. She was one of my favorite teachers in high school, and I've always looked back on her with fondness, even after that whole *Oedipus* debacle.

We look at teachers as if they're on this whole other plain of existence, because aside from our families, teachers help shape our future personalities. But teachers, just like our parents, are also *people*. Mrs. Reynolds wasn't acting out of spite. She was easily offended, and that crept into her work. I didn't mean to offend anyone. But it taught me that you have to know your audience, and that's why the teachers always had a problem with the type of language I used, *especially* on an assignment. High school just wasn't the place for it. I wouldn't hand in a business proposal with swear words, would I? I know what you're thinking, but no, I wouldn't.

I also like to think that I challenged my teachers as much as they challenged me. What I was doing, incorporating adult elements into my school papers and projects, asking if this were acceptable when I probably should have known better – they didn't come across that too often. And what was more puzzling to them was that I was a good student. I wasn't goofing off in the middle of class, interrupting the teacher in order to call attention to myself. I did it creatively through my assignments. I like to look at it as a two-for-one special.

Take that as you will, but ultimately, I survived high school with an A average, and I had three short films on my resume. When I attended film school in the fall, for better or worse, I'd have something to show people.

CHAPTER 9:

Film School and Attack of the B Movies

By the time of graduation, I was set on going into film. That's all I wanted to do. I loved the experience of making movies.

Let's not be pretentious. Aside from *Star Whores*, easily the worst of the three films, the videos were created out of necessity for school. I suppose *Oedipus* shows *some* artistic merit, but I still didn't know anything about how to craft a movie. When I watched movies, they were just entertainment. I didn't know what to look for in terms of cinematography, camera placement, lighting, or writing.

I couldn't see the point of paying for a four-year university when it was clear where I was headed. I was certain that I'd have to leave Michigan. The two film schools I was looking at were the New York Film Academy and the University of Southern California, which was George Lucas's alma mater. But aside from the expense of actually moving to these two locations, these schools weren't cheap.

Then I received a brochure in the mail for a film school located in Michigan, and it was about twenty minutes from home. My parents were skeptical, as I was. First of all, it was a one-year program. I found out later that was common with trade schools.

And they didn't offer a degree, but a certificate of achievement. It was also the only affordable option.

My parents didn't want me to *stop* making movies, but they warned me that it might be hard to make a living at it, given that at the time, Michigan had no film incentives, and nothing was happening here industry-wise. They encouraged me to go into broadcasting. But broadcasting isn't filmmaking. They use a lot of the same techniques and equipment, but I wanted to tell stories.

I argued that filmmaking was my passion, and that's what I wanted to do. I couldn't think of anything else I wanted more. I didn't want to work in retail like my mom, and I certainly didn't want to be a mechanic, regardless of the money. So, I enrolled at the Motion Picture Institute of Michigan. By that summer, I got my acceptance letter.

◆ ◆ ◆

Dan had two more years of school before he'd be a free man. That summer, he invited me to go on a family trip to South Dakota. It would be him, his parents, his sister, her best friend, and me. I was ecstatic. Apart from traveling to Florida and Ontario, I barely ever left Michigan. And with my parents' marriage rapidly crumbling, my dad's health getting worse, and their arguments becoming all the more toxic, I needed a week's vacation.

I never went on a long road trip before, but with my dad's trusty video camera, I made sure to document everything. The problem was, like an idiot, I left the camera charger at home, so once the battery ran out, I was shit out of luck. But I did get a piece of video that I'm quite proud of. Dan, if you're reading this, you know exactly what I'm referring to.

Dan's dad was a nice guy, but like a lot of dads, he had a short temper and he blew up easily. When he got frustrated, he tended to complain about anything and everything. But sometimes, during one of his rants, he would accidentally say something funny. As we passed through the heavy rush hour of Chicago (my first and only time driving through there), he noticed that we were surrounded by two things: taxi cabs and sunflowers. During a spout of road rage that involved honking his horn and giving other drivers the finger, he muttered, "God damn sunflowers are all over the fucking highway. They're probably from all the damn taxi drivers spitting out their sunflower seeds into traffic." I don't think I ever laughed so hard in my life.

But that's not what I caught on video. Dan and his younger sister, Jenny, had a typical sibling rivalry. It wasn't toxic, but they bickered a lot. On our way through the country, we made several stops at ShopKo, a chain of retail stores. At one of the stops, Dan bought a poster of a swimsuit model, to the annoyance of his sister.

As soon as Dan got back in the car, he took the poster out of its plastic. That was his first mistake. His second mistake was putting the poster in the backseat where Jenny had access to it.

We were all getting antsy, and at one point, Dan started aggravating the hell out of his sister and her friend. I decided I needed something interesting to film, for my latest documentary, *Three Losers in a Durango*. As most people do when a camcorder is pointed at them, Jenny and her friend got defensive and camera-shy. To make sure I couldn't get them on video, Jenny started to unravel Dan's poster.

Dan's dad was already beyond agitated with all the ruckus going on behind him. This was 2001, before GPS units were commonplace. Navigating anywhere was a headache, and the whole trip, Dan's parents were trying to figure out how to get us to our destination.

When Dan saw that Jenny was unraveling his precious poster, he lost it. "DON'T! DON'T DO THAT!"

That's when Dan's dad lost it. "SO HELP ME GOD, DANNY, IF YOU YELL LIKE THAT AGAIN!"

"Dad, they're ruining my poster!"

"Oh, that'll be real nice if it gets shriveled up, Jenny."

"It DIDN'T, *dad.*"

I've held on to that piece of footage since the day it happened. And whenever I think about Dan's dad (I still see him pop up on Facebook once in a while), I post that clip.

When it comes to my creativity, either my writing or my filmmaking, I don't discard anything. Everything I've ever done, from the very first *Galactic Redemption,* I've saved in storage, either on a physical hard drive, compact disc, or up in the Cloud. Occasionally it's nice to look back at the things I've done and say, *this is my life's work. This is what I've done.* Even if none of it goes beyond YouTube, it's proof that I existed. And it's nice to look back at those old videos and see how far I've come with my filmmaking.

Everything I've recorded on video is available for easy access on a couple of portable hard drives. When someone complains about how sucky life is (because life gives us no shortage of things to complain about), I pull up one of my old tapes. Tapes no one knew I still had, until I post a clip on Facebook showing them how they used to be. I probably have more videos of my friends than their parents do. It's kind of creepy, when you think about it.

When we finally got to South Dakota, it was breathtaking. We were surrounded by mountains. At certain points, you could look out and see for tens of miles in every direction. I won't lie, driving down those mountainous roads was terrifying, and thankfully, this was in the summer. God forbid someone tries making that trip when the roads ice over.

We stayed at a really nice resort. At the bottom of the hill, there was a lake, a mountain trail, and a little gift shop that sold the world's most kick-ass root beer. Dan and I must have spent all our traveling money on those root beers.

One morning, I got up early, when everyone was still asleep. I thought I'd go down for an hour and walk around the lake by myself. There were tons of people out and about that morning. I figured, what the hell? I could use some "me" time.

When I got down to the lake, I started following the trail around, and I saw this little detour. There was a sign that read, "Hiking trail – hike at your own risk". To this day, I have no idea what was on my mind. But I decided to hike at my own risk.

It was a trail that kept going down in one direction. Occasionally, I would come across some other hikers. The scenery was beautiful, and the cool, crisp morning air made it more wonderful. There's a certain fresh scent you get when you're around mountains, in the middle of nature. I was loving it. I was suddenly reminded that in a couple of days, I'd be back home again, in shitty-ass Michigan. I didn't want to go back.

As I looked at my watch, I realized I'd been gone for an hour. That meant that by the time I got back to the top of the trail, I would have been gone for at least two. I was praying that everyone was either still asleep or waking up by the time I got back.

What I didn't consider was, when you climb back up, it takes twice as long, because you're fighting gravity the whole way. My legs started to cave, and at such a high altitude it gets harder to breathe.

By the time I got back to our room, I was gone for three hours. That was more than enough time for Dan's parents to form a search party, begin calling the cops, and call my parents, pronouncing me dead.

I had never seen Dan's mom smoke before, and before my disappearing act, I'm sure it had been a while before she picked up a cigarette. I went back up to the room, where it was now empty, and started to worry because I knew they were out looking for me. I looked out the window, and sure enough, the entire party was standing in the parking lot, making frantic phone calls. It was then that I realized: a little note would have been nice. I waved down to them.

I remember Dan's mom's words clearly: "You're in big trouble, mister."

Of course, they were worried about me. They invited me to go on this trip, and I repaid them by going missing for three hours. If something happened to me, they would have been held responsible. But Dan's dad didn't yell at me, and they didn't lecture me or hold me hostage until we got back to Michigan. They were relieved that I was okay. I told them where I went, and that afternoon, I took them down that same trail myself. We probably would have spent the day in our room had I not ventured out. I should get kudos for being so adventurous, right?

Okay, it was an asshole thing to do. And I have no idea why it crossed my mind to do such a thing. If I may make a *Forrest Gump* reference – because that is one of my favorite films – I think maybe it was about putting the past behind me. It sounds pretentious as hell, I know. Here I was, just out of high school, in another state with friends, and adventuring out on my own. It was only a couple of miles, but it was something I experienced on my own. I made that decision. I took a leap of faith. And I was okay at the end of it. I think that's what that whole trip was about.

◆ ◆ ◆

Now that I was back home, my parents were on my case to get a job. Mom got me an interview at her grocery store, Farmer Jack. Farmer Jack was a family-owned company that operated in Michigan for seventy years. Then one day, a big corporation came along and bought them out, and everything turned to shit. Many years later, I was hired in.

My mom got a kick out of the fact that I was working at the same place she was. I started out bagging groceries, schlepping in carts and mopping floors. The employees were okay, but the clientele got on my fucking nerves. Anyone who's had to work with the general public knows how frustrating the average customer is. And the lower on the totem pole you are, the worse it gets. So many customers treated me like an A-1 retard. I can't count how many times a customer, usually some old hag with a cane, instructed me to not smash their bread, and to please put their eggs at the top of the cart. It was humiliating.

My manager was this huge ball-breaker. If I clocked in from my break two minutes late, she was right there to say something. If she caught me eating a small snack by the check lanes, she went on the intercom and made a loud chewing noise so the whole store could hear her.

It was worse when I became a cashier, because I was stuck in one spot all day long. Often times, I would beg to go out and gather carts because I couldn't take dealing with the rude customers for hours on end. And when I was outside, I would daydream about making movies. I was an up-and-coming film-maker, in a warehouse with a small film crew. We built models for the *Galactic Redemption* movie, spaceships and weapons, and alien creatures, like the cantina scene from *A New Hope*. We were swigging down Mountain Dew, working into the wee hours of the night, and excited as all hell because we were living the dream: we were making a movie.

I always felt degraded when I worked a retail job (and there were many of them throughout the years), because even though I was able to pay for school, I wasn't working in my field. It was soul-crushing.

◆ ◆ ◆

The only silver lining was that I'd be starting at MPI in September. I sat down with the Dean, the guy who co-founded the school, a local filmmaker named Doug. He and his partner, Kurt, made their own feature film in the early 90's, a cult hor-ror film called *Hellmaster.* Through their own connections, they were able to get B-movie actors John Saxon and David Emge, and they sold the film to one of the big cable networks. They opened the film school because they believed you didn't need a four-year degree to get into filmmaking, and they promised a completely hands-on experience – none of that film theory nonsense.

They put me on a payment plan, which meant I wouldn't be able to earn my certificate until I paid off the balance in full. I also needed to come up with some cash up-front, so they could secure a seat for me. Dad loaned me the initial first payment, but after that, I worked my ass off at Farmer Jack, saving every penny so I could make my payments on time.

When they said the school was all hands-on, they weren't kidding. From the first day, we were on a mock film set, running cameras, striking lights, recording sound, and running through scripts. The way it worked was, we had several classes geared toward specific areas of filmmaking – either lighting, cinematography, screenwriting, directing, film financing, sound recording, or script continuity. We were broken up into several groups, and every couple of weeks, we'd rotate to different stations. We were all learning at a rapid-fire pace, and it was exhilarating.

I was one of the youngest students there. Mostly everyone else was in their mid-20's to mid-30's, and they either had families or were looking to switch fields. But we all loved movies. It was great to have that in common. I don't think there was one person I didn't get along with. They all knew I was young, fresh out of high school, but we had common interests. Often times, they would recommend movies for me to watch, and we'd always discuss our favorite filmmakers, our favorite movies, new movies that were coming out – it was a blast.

Built into the tuition cost, each student was given five hundred feet of 16mm motion picture film. This was when I realized I was in *film* school. The days of running around with my dad's shoddy 8mm camcorder were over. This was the real deal.

If you don't know much about how movies are made, or why shooting on film was a big deal, here's the scoop: from the late 19th century up until the beginning of the 21st century, movies were traditionally shot on film. Even before the advent of video tape, if you wanted to shoot home movies, you shot on rolls of 8mm film, then sent the film to your local drugstore to get developed, like you would with a standard roll of film from a still camera. The thing was, as good as film looked, it was cost prohibitive for most aspiring filmmakers.

Motion picture film is sold by the foot, and that adds up when you realize that film is shot at 24 frames per second. If film stock costs seventy-five cents per foot, and a foot of 35mm film amounts to about 12 frames – do the math. Imagine paying a dollar for every second of film you shoot. This is a rough estimate, but when you factor in the additional costs of developing the film, it's probably not that far off track. That's one of the reasons digital filmmaking, once considered a niche market, gained a lot of traction at the turn of the century. As editing software became more powerful and more accessible, filmmakers started turning out in droves. The industry had to change to meet this demand, and today, as far as I know, most productions are shot digitally, in 4K. The cost of the equipment is through the roof, but if you want to make a film on your own, there has been no better time to be a filmmaker.

Motion picture film looks great, and for many years, until the advent of 4K came along, nothing could match its pristine look. Film has a certain cinematic feel that not even the early HD cameras could capture faithfully. But film also has its disadvantages. First, you can't just rewind it to see what you've got. You have to send it to the lab to be processed, and in the best-case scenario, you don't get the footage back until the next day.

Film doesn't record sound, so you have the problem of having to sync your audio to the picture, which is why most film productions have that clapboard. Most productions still shoot this way, because in order to capture decent audio, you really need a separate sound source. But with film, there isn't any sound until you've synced it up with the correct audio file.

As a physical medium, film can also be tricky. Film is extremely sensitive to light, which is why you're not supposed to run unexposed film through the x-ray machines at the airport. There have probably been so many film productions that have lost days of shooting because of this. Also, in order to load the film into the camera, you have to do so in a dark environment, usually in a black bag specifically made for this purpose. This means that when you load the film, you have to do it purely by touch. If any light gets to the film before it gets developed, the entire roll will be overexposed. To learn this skill, our instructors gave us rolls of overexposed film stock, and we'd practice threading the film in the light before taking timed tests, where we'd have to load the film in darkness. I wasn't especially skilled at this.

Lighting for film is a huge undertaking. Today, I see most filmmakers setting up their lights according to how they want their scene to look. But with film, it isn't enough to get the scene to look good. You need to know how much light is required in order to get a decent exposure. This means you need to use a specialized tool called a light meter to get a reading of how much light is on your subject. You use that information to adjust the aperture of your camera accordingly.

In other words, shooting on film was a giant undertaking. It's no wonder George Lucas was pushing for a new, digital medium. Shooting on film was akin to shooting a still photograph in the early 1900's, when you'd make everyone stand still for twenty minutes in order to get a decent shot. It seemed like such a slow process. I missed the days of running around my high school, grabbing shots and moving on.

Most of my time in the program was spent trying to come up with an idea to use as my thesis project, the thing we were all gearing up for. Five hundred feet of 16mm film equated to about 12 minutes of footage. That included retakes and do-overs, so I'd have to be conservative. I couldn't do a 35-minute action figure film with those limitations.

The first script I wrote was essentially a film version of *Leon's Tragedy,* called *Lust and Friendship.* It was darker in tone, and I was trying to be more subjective with it, examining both sides of the story and acknowledging that my protagonist wasn't the hapless victim I portrayed him to be in the past.

The reason I scrapped this one was because there were too many factors: lots of locations, plus the script called for fog and rain, elements that were difficult to create. I also realized that with the cost of film, even 16mm short ends, which was my cheapest route, I wasn't going to be able to afford anything past the initial 500 feet. My script was well over twenty pages, equating to a twenty-minute film, at least. Not to mention, to pull off the kind of drama the script asked for, I would need a hell of a cast, and you learn quickly that the good actors expect to get paid.

The next script was inspired by the place I worked, a place I still describe as Hell on Earth. The title was *Savings Time*, derived from Farmer Jack's little commercial jingle: "It's always savings time at Farmer Jack." If you're from Michigan, that should ring a bell.

With this one, I wrote several drafts of the script, broke the script down – this is the process where you get the budget and the shooting schedule together – and I even storyboarded the entire film using still photos I shot with Dan.

There was quite a bit of Romero's *Dawn of the Dead*, here. The concept was that consumers are really no different than mindless zombies, and in the film, we would have literally seen that transformation. The protagonist is a cashier named Norb, who spends all night long ringing up customers. As the night goes on, each of Norb's customers gets stranger and stranger, until Norb's final customer is the literal interpretation of what we call a zombie – scars, bloody make-up, the works. The zombie bites Norb, and then exits the scene. Norb, now at the end of his shift, walks out to his car and pulls out a gun from his glove compartment, shooting himself in the head. This would have been an especially tricky, yet awesome effects shot, with blood spattering all over the windshield. The film concludes with Norb exiting the vehicle, now a zombie himself, as he grabs a shopping cart and heads into the store.

I would have loved to shoot this film, but the corporate entity wouldn't let me shoot in the grocery store. Farmer Jack was a corporate chain, and big corporations have issues with camcorders inside their establishments, even after hours. One time, my brother Jack needed to film a school project inside that same location. He got the go-ahead from management, because it was a much smaller project, but a lot of customers were upset when they saw us walking around recording things. What, were they afraid they were going to end up on the 6:00 news?

The store manager was okay with it, provided we shot after store hours and we paid for anything we broke. But he had to get clearance from upper management. That meant that I had to send them a copy of the script. Well, shit.

I improvised. I wrote a special "PG" version of the script that eliminated all the zombie references. Now, it was just Norb ringing up customers. Even after censoring myself, I got turned down by the public relations department, who was afraid the overall scope of the project would reflect poorly on the company.

I could have looked around for another location, a mom-and-pop grocery store, but I was anxious, and I was running out of time. Once again, I was working on a deadline. I needed to have a concept locked down, and my first two ideas sank.

What I was really trying to do was expand my work beyond my house. Aside from *Short Future*, everything I'd ever shot was at my home. I shot every room in my house a dozen times. I was in film school. I wanted to go beyond what was available to me.

I was also jealous that some of the other students were getting cool locations for their projects. One girl got access to an entire nightclub. Remember, a lot of these students had disposable income, so they could afford to spend a few extra bucks in order to ramp up their films' production values. I was still paying off my tuition, not to mention trying to make my movie for as little money as possible. But aside from Farmer Jack, I didn't have access to any other location. Everyone I knew who had a job worked at some big corporate place.

Then it hit me: write what you know. Just because I was in film school didn't mean I had to make the next *Jaws*. It didn't even mean I had to craft something spectacular. It just needed to be better than what I'd done before, which in all honesty shouldn't have been that hard. Hey, I was going to shoot on film. That had to count for something.

What I decided to do was an homage to everything I'd done before. All my films were inspired by *Star Wars*, *Friday the 13th*, *Nightmare on Elm Street*, and others. How cool would it be to do a fun, popcorn movie that nodded to all those things? If you ever attempt to watch a student film, whether good or bad, you might notice that most of them seem very personal. I wanted to do something that was a little more accessible to people. It wasn't the most cinematic idea, but I wanted to enjoy the experience of making a movie.

The result was *Attack of the B Movies*, a story of a working-class couch potato who falls asleep while watching all these great B-movies, then wakes up and finds himself in his own B-movie universe!

As far as the horror films are concerned, sure, they can be considered B-movies, if not in a loose sense. But whenever *Star Wars* comes up, people ask me, "Really? Is *Star Wars* considered a B-movie?"

B-movies are traditionally thought of as low-budgeted versions of big Hollywood blockbusters; *Sharknado* as opposed to *Jaws*. In a very broad sense, sure. I'm sure you've heard the term "B-movie actor", which applies to celebrities like Bruce Campbell, John Saxon, and Julie Strain, all of whom have built their careers making cult films, or B-movies.

But the B-movie used to be the other part of a double-feature. You might have the mega-budgeted, sweeping epic starring Clark Gable and Ava Gardner – that was your "A" movie – preceded by a swashbuckling action-adventure starring Joey No-Name. These were typically your Westerns, or your genre films.

When describing *Indiana Jones*, George Lucas often referred to those films as old-fashioned B-movies because of their fast-paced styles and 1930's settings; and those were all huge movies!

So, I decided to group *Star Wars* into that category. After all, the name of the first film is *Episode IV*, because it starts right in the middle of the action. And doesn't *Star Wars* borrow from a lot of the great genre films? Westerns and Japanese mythologies?

Unfortunately, I was once again limited to the only location I had ready access to – my house. My parents were fine with it. What did they care? I shot all my other movies there. But I don't think they realized the scope of this production.

This wasn't going to be me and some friends running around with a little camcorder. This was going to be a crew – a skeleton crew, but a crew nonetheless – taking over the house for an entire weekend, while lugging around this big 20-pound film camera, boxes of lighting equipment, and a fog machine. Not to mention, I was going to have a make-up department.

The script called for the main protagonist to be male, and someone who was preferably athletic. There was going to be a lot of running away from things. Jason was going to be in the movie, along with Freddy Krueger, some zombies, as well as a cameo from Luke Skywalker and Darth Vader. And it also called for a little girl, someone for the protagonist to try and save. She was directly inspired by the girl on the tricycle in *Nightmare on Elm Street 3*. What this all meant was, I was going to need some make-up, for Jason and the zombies in particular. I wasn't sure how I was going to pull off Freddy, because the consumer make-up they sold at Party City always looked terrible. I also needed some blood. There was also a scene in which the protagonist, called "Rico" in the script, shoots Jason with a Winchester rifle. So, I needed to figure out how to pull off squibs, or fake bullet wounds, for those with their fingers far from the pulse of the filmmaking community.

I was also going to need actors. This was a film where I truly wanted to be behind the camera. I wanted to *direct* the actors for a change, not *be* the actor. I looked high and low for someone to be Jason, but all the other students were busy working on their own thesis projects.

Then I figured, who better to play Jason than Kane Hodder?

Well, I couldn't get Kane Hodder, so my second choice was Yours Truly. That's right, I would once again be directing from in front of the camera. It only made sense; out of eighteen years' worth of Halloweens, I went as Jason for at least half of those years. I knew how to craft the perfect mask, and I knew which Jason I wanted to emulate – C.J. Graham from *Jason Lives*.

As far as the rest of the cast, the film school held an open casting call in downtown Royal Oak. Each of us brought our video cameras so we could record the various performances from the local gathering of talent. As usual, we split into groups, and we each grabbed an area of Woody's Diner that would suit our auditions.

How auditioning works is, the director, or whoever's running the audition, will give out *sides* to those trying out for the roles. Sides are little segments either written specifically for the audition, or grabbed from the script, usually a couple pages in length.

At the time, I knew my film wasn't going to have that much to offer in the way of acting – it was mainly a grown man running from things. But I really wanted to get a wide range from these actors. They were coming here, anyway, so I may as well put them to work.

There was still a little bit of that rambunctious, rebellious quality left over from high school. I don't know what came over me, because in film school, I was typically the introvert. I decided to write my own sides, but not based on anything from *B Movies* – it was more or less inspired from *Savings Time*. But nothing in *Savings Time* came remotely close to the kind of dialogue I'd prepared for my actors. In case you're wondering – yes, after all these years, I still have the original audition footage. So here, for you, is the full transcript of that audition:

CASHIER: (yawns) How ya doing?

PREGNANT CUSTOMER: I know you've probably had a rough night, but don't you think it's rude to yawn in front of somebody? Didn't your mom teach you to look away when you do things like that?

CASHIER: All my mom ever told me was that if she found any cum stains on my underwear, she wasn't cleaning them.

PREGNANT CUSTOMER: Charming. Are you going to start ringing up these groceries? Or are we just going to stand around here, bullshitting until closing time?

CASHIER: Aren't we getting a little testy?

PREGNANT CUSTOMER: Look at me. I'm not exactly fit to lift things.

CASHIER: Maybe if you did some actual work, instead of sitting around the house getting knocked up, you wouldn't feel so bad.

PREGNANT CUSTOMER: Excuse me? What kind of bull-shit comment is that, you freaky little mongoloid? I want to talk to your manager right now.

CASHIER: No. She doesn't want to talk to you.

PREGNANT CUSTOMER: And why is that?

CASHIER: She's like me.

PREGNANT CUSTOMER: And how is that?

CASHIER: We both think you're a total cunt.
PREGNANT CUSTOMER: Listen, asshole. I'm a pregnant

woman. How dare you talk to me like that!

CASHIER: I'm a tired employee, and I'm sick of your constant bitching.

PREGNANT CUSTOMER: Where is your manager?

CASHIER: She's on vacation.

PREGNANT CUSTOMER: Where is your manager? Where the FUCK is your manager?

CASHIER: Listen, bitch. I know your tight ass thinks you're all high and mighty, but I could give a shit about your condition. And until I do, just fuck off!

PREGNANT CUSTOMER: Fuck this!

Keep in mind, there were a lot of little kids waiting in line to read for these filmmakers. But a lot of these actors really got into their roles. And when it was time for them to read from my sides, they were excited that they were going to be able to perform something with a little stank to it. They really got into it. You could hear the f-bombs clearly across the room, and at times, there were a hundred people there. Our station immediately turned heads – everyone wanted to know what kind of film we were making.

Intermittently, we'd have to take a break for the kiddies. Obviously, they couldn't read my sides, so I'd have them sing a little song. But it was especially funny hearing two grown men cuss each other out, only to transition to a cute little five-year-old sing "Itsy Bitsy Spider" thirty seconds later.

I ended up choosing two actors from the entire audition: an established local actor, Devin, and a child actress named Kerry. To be fair, I chose Devin mainly because he was – well, an established actor. I saw him in a previous short film, and heard that he worked with some of the MPI staff.

Kerry, like all the other child actors, came in and sang a song – a hearty rendition of "Tomorrow" from *Annie*. However, fellow classmate Anton, who was sort of my producer, was also interested in casting Kerry for *his* project, so we teamed up and shared her for both of our films.

Anton was invaluable. Not only did we cast together, but he also stuck around while we did taped rehearsals of the script. I figured since I wasn't much of an artist, I would invite Devin and Kerry over so they could do a quick run-through of the entire film, which I would shoot on my dad's 8mm camcorder. The resulting video, once edited together, would serve as my animatics. It worked out fine, for the sake of blocking and camera positioning, but I couldn't get anyone to take the work seriously.

To put it mildly, Devin was a bit of a smartass, and there was a sense that he didn't want to be there. He wasn't getting paid, for one – which is something the actors were told when they auditioned – but he always seemed to have a snide remark ready to go.

We were rehearsing the opening scene, which has Devin sitting on the couch, flipping through channels. When making a film, the sequence goes like this: the director calls out, "Roll camera." The camera operator starts up the camera, and responds, "Camera rolling." Next, the director usually calls out, "Roll sound." The sound engineer begins recording the audio, and responds by saying, "Speed." The clapper will then briefly enter the shot with the clapboard, announce the scene and take number, state, "Marker," then clap the slate (this is how the editor syncs the audio to picture in the editing room). Once the clapper exits the frame, that's when the director usually calls, "Action!", signaling for the actors to begin their scene. It seems like a drawn-out process, but the whole sequence takes about ten seconds.

I was still getting used to working in that kind of professional environment. I was nervous because it was late, and there were family members watching in the background, so I was conscious that I had an audience and it added to the tension. As I was getting ready to film the rehearsal, I pushed "record" on the camcorder – but I forgot to tell Devin. A few seconds went by, and finally Devin said, "Most directors say 'Action'."

To be fair to Devin, I *did* misrepresent my film during the auditions. Not that he seemed that enthused to begin with, but the sides I used for the audition were an attention grabber, and most of the actors enjoyed reading those lines. When I called Devin and asked him to be the lead in the film, he didn't know that I was shooting this goofy horror spoof, in which he'd have virtually no dialogue. When Devin's on the couch yawning, he's probably not doing a whole lot of acting. It wasn't that interesting a part.

Also, because I was spending a lot of time blocking the scenes, Devin couldn't stay for the duration of the rehearsal process, so I used friends, namely Anton and Dan, to fill in.

At this point I met Matt, who remains a close friend. I met him through Dan, shortly after our trip to South Dakota. Matt went to a different school, and lived quite a way from us, but somehow, through this weird inner-circle, Dan and he crossed paths and hit it off.

When I first met Matt, he asked where I worked, to which I replied, "Farmer Jack-Off." From then on, Matt stuck around. We enjoyed each other's sense of humor.

But Matt was also extremely high-strung. If you got him in a room with a group of mellow dudes, it would take about thirty seconds before everyone was bouncing off the walls, just because he had that kind of energy.

It was fun at first. Meeting Matt was like meeting someone's kid after he'd been fed a gallon of sugar. But that aspect of him quickly wore me down. It didn't help that I invited him over to help with the rehearsals, and all he wanted to do was goof off, making jokes about paying taxes and throwing my dirty work gloves at the camera. It was frustrating.

Years later, Matt, Dan and I got together frequently and

made a ton of videos together. But they weren't filmmakers. They didn't care about putting in the time and the effort. They enjoyed the process of running around with a video camera and shooting things. That's what Dan and I did in Video Production in high school.

Shooting *Attack of the B Movies* wasn't all fun. In fact, I don't think I had fun the entire time I was shooting. From day one of production, it felt like work. It felt like something I was making in order to fulfill a school requirement. In other words, it was just like high school, with more equipment and no teacher to tell me, "You can't use the word 'porn'."

On the weekend of the shoot, my parents' living room was littered with metal boxes filled with lighting equipment, sound and camera gear, rolls of film, and tangled up extension cords. It was like moving into a dorm. Many independent film-makers compare making a movie to asking your friends to help you move. And that's a reasonable comparison.

You never shoot a location exactly the way it's given to you. You modify it to fill the needs of your movie. I've never been good at this (because I'm always limited to my goddamn house), but typically furniture needs to be moved, ordinary household items need to be relocated so they're not in certain shots, and in some cases, if you have the budget, you might even have to change the light fixtures and repaint the entire location – although we didn't go to that extreme. It's all about filling the needs of the story. The next time you watch a movie, pay close attention to the environments. If there's a scene in a house – very common in movies – a set designer and an art department had to plan how to make it look good on film. Normal houses, no matter how extravagant, aren't that cinematic until you light them a certain way. Pay attention to things in the background, such as wall décor, picture frames – a thousand little decisions that have to be made about a set that you'll probably only see for a couple seconds.

The other thing to consider is camera placement. Just because you plan out your angles doesn't mean you're going to be able to place the camera wherever you want. Sacrifices might have to be made. It's hard to explain this unless you've been on a film set, but you might have this great idea for a shot, only to get stuck because you don't have the room you need to maneuver. Usually, it's a quick fix, like moving a table away from a back wall. But these are all considerations you have to factor in when you get to the set.

Today, cameras come in so many different sizes, and even cell phones take decent enough video, if you have the proper lighting conditions and some sort of tripod. But a film camera is a pretty cumbersome piece of equipment, and sometimes it takes two people just to move it around – one person to mount it on their shoulders, and someone else to help guide that person around set while they're filming.

There are perfectionists who will stop at nothing to make sure everything is perfect before they pull off their first shot. A lot of students blazed through their initial five hundred feet of film stock in seconds, because they planned on buying more. I didn't have that option. I had to make each second count. If something wasn't perfect, too bad. I had to move on.

I storyboarded most of the film, and this was great, because while Anton took on partial directing duties, I was in the make-up chair. I partnered up with fellow classmate Mark, who was into make-up effects. We went to Party City and for about twenty bucks got everything we needed; liquid latex, a bald cap, and green make-up for Jason; fake blood; not to mention some rubber scars for the zombies. We also bought a can of fog juice, which we needed for our fog machine. We were only going to use it for one scene, but it seems with fog, you either go all-out, or you don't use it at all. I tried using the fog in moderation, but for as little use as we got out of it, it would have been better to eliminate the fog altogether.

It took Mark about two hours to get me in the Jason makeup. However, we kept falling behind schedule. We shot on a cloudy day, so it kept sprinkling, which was problematic for the makeup. It also got dark quickly, so when you watch those outside scenes, nothing matches up. One second it's light out, and then it's nighttime. And because I was desperately trying to capture as much as I could, I pushed back all my scenes to the end of the night. For three days, I walked around in full makeup, directing the movie and not getting anything shot with myself until later in the day.

The one bit I was excited for was getting shot with the Winchester rifle. The rifle was a cheap plastic toy. When Devin goes to pick it up from the garage, it plays out comically, because the rifle is so petite in Devin's meaty grip.

We taped a garden hose inside my costume, where the end of it protruded from a slit inside my clothes. The practical effects guy, Jeremy, stood off-camera with a pump that was loaded with fake blood. Once I yelled "Action," Jeremy pushed down on the pump, and blood ejected from my costume. It looked cool, even though it probably didn't spatter in the right direction. I wasn't a Forensics major, after all.

During the third day of the shoot, I ran around frantically trying to rearrange scenes. I was almost out of film, and I only shot half of what I intended. This was the only day we'd have Kerry on set, and with child actors, you have to be careful because there are strict laws restricting how long they can work each day. Not to mention, Kerry had other gigs going on throughout the day, so we had to push all of her scenes to the front of the schedule. There was this big escape scene in my basement (the one area of my house I hadn't actually shot in) where Jason chases Devin and Kerry right into this thin corridor filled with zombies. Trapped, they leave the corridor, only to come face-to-face with Yours Truly. Jason then stabs Kerry, leaving Devin to exact revenge by kneeing me in the crotch. He says, "Ten sequels, and all it takes is a kick in the nuts to take you out?" Devin kept wanting to redo the scene, substituting the word "nuts" with other colorful nouns.

The last thing we shot was the epic climax, where Devin runs out of the house and confronts Luke Skywalker and Darth Vader, who are battling it out on my front lawn. It was a quick shoot, with hardly any choreography. I directed the actors to repeatedly bash each other with lightsabers, and then have Vader stab Luke, winning the fight. Then Devin was supposed to go crazy, as if he was imagining the whole thing.

As we filmed the last scene, the camera made a loud "click-click-click" sound, signifying that we used up our last roll of film. Alas, the final shot couldn't be filmed, unless I could somehow manage to buy another roll of film.

I didn't intend to shoot for another weekend. What I had was going to have to do. I was bumming hard. I compromised the entire script, deleting half the scenes I intended to shoot. I had no idea how I was going to piece it together, and I had no money to buy more film. I did the best I could, but suffice to say, I was discouraged. I was starting to see why my parents tried to get me to steer toward broadcasting. Maybe filmmaking just wasn't for me.

We packed everything up that night, including the three rolls of film we shot that weekend. A week later, I got the film negative back, along with a VHS tape that contained all my footage. I waited in anticipation to see how it came out, expecting nothing to be in focus and everything to be underexposed.

Two of the three rolls of film looked fine. But the third roll came with a note. The film magazine was loaded incorrectly. The film didn't have enough slack when it was threaded inside the magazine, and it rubbed up against the gate, getting an improper exposure. The result was five minutes of static. My entire third day was a total loss. The basement scene, along with the lightsaber fight and the climax, hadn't been filmed. I never missed my dad's camcorder more than that moment. Yes, the picture quality was terrible, but at least you got a picture when you were done filming.

I had no idea what I was going to do. I went home to watch the footage that *did* come out, and it looked good. But there wasn't enough there to tell a story. I was forced to omit too many scenes to save on costs and losing an entire day of shooting cut deep.

While in school, we had this debate about the possibilities of shooting digitally. At that time, I don't think many of us understood the difference between shooting on a digital camcorder, and doing the kind of digital photography that George Lucas was using on his upcoming *Star Wars* movie, *Attack of the Clones*. First off, Lucas was pioneering these cameras from scratch, partnering with professional companies to get the desired look. And he was shooting in high-def, which, believe it or not, was a fresh industry term in those days. There was nothing on the consumer market that came anywhere close to what Lucas was doing. The first consumer HD camcorders didn't start rolling out until around 2005, and even then, they were expensive.

But maybe it was an option. My dad purchased a mini-DV camcorder. It wasn't anything special, but it was still light-years ahead of that dusty old 8mm camera, which by now was on its last leg. Most of the footage got damaged, because the camcorder ate the tapes while recording. My dad's purchase was a godsend.

I told Doug about my financial situation, and asked him if I could finish shooting my film using digital video. He said as long as more than half of the project was shot on film, he didn't have a problem with it.

This actually worked out in my favor. Now, all I had to concern myself with was buying the mini-DV tapes (about twenty bucks for a pack), as well as scheduling the reshoots. That proved problematic, because Kerry and Devin moved on to other projects.

Fortunately, they were able to give up one weekend so I could finish the film, about three months after the initial shoot. I had to look at the footage to make sure they wore the exact same clothes. I didn't want a repeat of the *Short Future* incident. I had to go out, buy more makeup, and once again tear apart my parents' house. By this time, they were more than slightly agitated. Even though I wasn't shooting on film, I still used the same lighting package, and I was still recording sound externally, so that I got the same quality of audio across the entire film.

By the end of that rushed, yet productive weekend, I had two cassette tapes filled with all-new footage that I could splice with my film footage to get a somewhat finished movie.

How I used to edit was, I shot out of sequence, as is the case with most movies, and then I dumped the raw footage from the 8mm cassette to a blank VHS tape; that became my "master". From there, I dumped that footage, in the proper sequence, onto a second blank tape. That meant I'd have to fast-forward or rewind my way around the tape, find the right sequence, push record on the second VCR, and pause every time I wanted to make a cut. This is what was known as *linear* editing.

Believe it or not, before editing software, this was how you edited a film – not so much with VCRs, but on editing beds. The editor ran the film through the editing bed, using a screen to monitor the footage. When the editor gets ready to perform a cut, he or she uses a razor blade to cut into the workprint, then scotch tapes the two pieces of film together – and there you have it, a simple cut. Repeat the process eight thousand more times, and you have yourself a finished film.

The drawback to this was, if you made a mistake, you couldn't hit the *undo* button. You'd have to go back, re-cut the footage, and make your change. You had to do it all in sequence. There was no jumping ahead to make changes. Likewise, with the two VHS tapes, if I made a mistake, I'd have to rewind the tape, and hope I didn't accidentally delete an important shot while making a new edit.

The term *non-linear editing* came about from computer software. If you make a mistake, you can hit the *undo* button as many times as you like. Don't like a specific shot? You can lift it off the timeline, and easily insert an alternate take. You can move entire sequences around just by dragging and dropping. The filmmaker has so much creative freedom nowadays.

Attack of the B Movies was the first film of mine that would be edited in this fashion. Today there are dozens of software packages available, the biggest examples being Adobe Premiere, Final Cut Pro, and Avid Media Composer. Back then, MPI used Avid, which is still the most widely-used software package for big film productions. We took a few quick courses in editing, but if you're new to the process, it can be overwhelming. In 2002, editing software wasn't quite mainstream yet. An Avid system alone cost thousands of dollars.

Because we were relying on the school's editing suite, we'd go home, watch our footage, and compose an EDL: an edit decision list. That's when you choose the best takes, and write down the SMPTE timecode in the order you want to make your cuts. When you head into the editing room, you're not wasting time searching through hours of footage, trying to find your best takes.

This was more complicated for me, because I had my 16mm footage, which had the appropriate timecode. But I also had my mini-DV footage, which used a different timecode format.

My editor was a guy named Jim, one of the MPI instructors. Jim single-handedly saved my movie. When we finally had a rough-cut assembled, I was worried because there were obvious story gaps that didn't make sense. Jim showed me how to repurpose footage to fill in those gaps. Footage that I thought was useless garbage was used to transition to the next scene.

There's this thing that happens with a film while you're editing that most audiences take for granted. At its earliest stages, a movie looks rough because all you're doing is laying out the proper sequence of events and getting a feel for the film's timing. That first cut is there to get an idea of the final runtime. But without the music, the sound effects, the dialogue, or the titles, all you're looking at is a sequence of clips.

Once we had an assembled rough-cut, and the audio was being synced up to the picture, it started coming together. At least now we had a plausible story. You could watch it from beginning to end and comprehend what was going on.

Next was the fun part: the sound effects. My sound library consisted of whatever I could find online, as well as clips from existing movies and video games. I didn't have a complete understanding of intellectual copyright law, and besides, this was going to be shown at a small film festival. It wasn't like I was making money off this. Rather than going out and recording the sound effects myself, which I didn't have the time for, I "borrowed" sounds from *Star Wars, Friday the 13th*, and even the *Resident Evil* games. To this day, when I sit down to play the original *Resident Evil* (a game I *still* haven't finished), I'll eventually hear a familiar zombie sound, only to realize that I used the exact soundbite in *B Movies*.

I also "borrowed" most of the music. The opening titles are from *The Blair Witch Project*, which used this haunting, echoing knocking sound. There are a ton of Manfredini cues from *Friday the 13th*, not to mention John Williams' Raiders March, which I used during the climactic lightsaber duel at the end. I even used footage from the movies themselves. During the opening scene, when Devin is thumbing through the channels, I cut back and forth between Devin and the TV, where you clearly see clips from *Dawn of the Dead, Dream Warriors, Friday the 13th*, and *The Empire Strikes Back*. The idea was to create parallels in my movie to the movie clips I showed the audience.

On a much smaller scale, the experience of putting together *Attack of the B Movies* was akin to what Lucas experienced when he was making the first *Star Wars*. While filming, I thought the movie was going to be a disaster. During editing, it started to come together, and everything worked out fine. For the watchful viewer, you can easily tell which footage was shot with film and which was digital, but surprisingly, we were able to match most of the shots. Even with all the continuity errors, it was something I grew proud of.

The film premiered that summer at the school's annual student film festival, which was our graduation day. They didn't pick some shitty A/V room and screen the films on some ancient television set. They rented out a theater at the Emagine in Novi. Our films were going to be projected on the big screen in front of two hundred people. I can't begin to tell you how exciting this was for a budding filmmaker.

They screened the films back-to-back. I was curious to see what everyone else did, because I didn't get to work on a lot of their films. That was one of the advantages to going to film school, was that you got to learn primarily by working on everyone else's film. But I missed out on a lot of that because I was so busy working, trying to pay off my tuition.

I had a hard time focusing on everyone else's film because I couldn't wait for mine to show up. And I'm sure everyone else felt the same way about their own film.

Finally, I heard the opening music, the track I stole from *Blair Witch*. For the next ten minutes, the audience was going to see what I spent the last three months making. I braced myself, wondering how people would react to it. Ten minutes is lengthy for a student film, when the average length is 3-5 minutes.

It had its share of laughs and applause. I think why people connected with it was, it's a fun movie. There's not a lot of intellect or heart. It doesn't say much about me, aside from the fact that I really love the kinds of movies represented. But it was a fun watch. People didn't have to guess the hidden meaning or look on, bored, when they didn't get the subject matter. The only regret I had was the end lightsaber sequence. I wished I took an effects course, so I could have animated the lightsabers. When the scene came up where Vader and Luke fight, and Devin, Jason, and two zombies look on with grave interest, the lightsabers look like exactly what they are – toy lightsabers that you buy off the clearance rack at Toys 'R Us. The sounds were there, the buzzing of the sabers, Vader's breathing, even Luke's famous scream when Vader stabs him in the stomach and wins the battle. But visually, the glowing sabers would have made that scene pop out more, especially considering how underexposed that scene was.

Over the next decade, I returned to my old films and tweaked them, using new techniques I picked up as an editor. Once I got a hold of some affordable editing equipment,

I scrapped the ancient word document titles from my high school films, and used the software to build better ones. In *Star Whores*, I created an opening crawl that better represented the ones seen in the *Star Wars* films, and I could do color correcting and transitions, smoothing them out and making them look *slightly* more polished. For *B Movies*, I went back and animated the lightsabers. It doesn't add much to the film, but the scene looks authentic.

Recently, I uploaded the original versions of the films, for several reasons.

For one, my tastes have changed. I used to love when directors added content to their films, thinking that more footage meant a better filmgoing experience. As I got older, I realized that usually, less is more. Watch those ridiculously long extended cuts of Peter Jackson's *Lord of the Rings* trilogy, an already long series of films. Some of those extended scenes are nice, but by the time you get to *Return of the King*, it feels like you're watching a mini-series.

The main reason I went back to the original cuts was that I wanted people to see the films as I originally made them, and see how much I've grown as a filmmaker. Regardless of which versions of the films you watch, it's obvious that *Attack of the B Movies* is a HUGE step up from *Short Future*. It was the first film I made that has a simple narrative structure. *Oedipus* is fine when you're shit-faced, but no audience, no matter how familiar they are with the source material, is going to understand that film. It wasn't designed to be a movie. It was a school project that I tried to turn into a film. When you see how far I've come not just with my filmmaking techniques, but also with the technology that's available, I think it's impressive to see the evolution.

I know I sound pretentious. These are small short films. But actual work went into them. I'm passionate about every movie I've made, even the bad ones, because I spent time on them. There's something there that I can show people. *Hey, I made this dopey little movie with Micro Machines action figures – it kinda sucks. Wanna watch it?* Chances are, most people would say sure. What do they have to lose? Trust me, there have been far worse films made, and mine are short.

The following year, I took *Attack of the B Movies* back to my alma mater, Berkley High School. I presented it to the video production class. It was funny, because the first thing my former teacher asked was if it was appropriate. I said that it was, but how would I really know what was appropriate? There's no swearing, no sexual references – except for when Jason gets kicked in the nuts – and minimal blood. It was a pure film in every respect. I even brought a roll of my 16mm negative, so the students could see that it was shot on film.

I then showed it to my former Language Arts teacher, Mrs. Reynolds. Her opinion mattered to me. I popped it in and sat there for ten minutes as she watched it. She had no reaction. She didn't stop it right in the middle and tell me it was garbage, but as the film played, I got more and more nervous.

When the credits rolled, she turned to me and said she was impressed. It was night-and-day from what I showed her the previous year. It looked like a *professional film*.

Attack of the B Movies didn't get me any jobs, and it wasn't awarded student film of the year. But it was a project that I worked hard to produce, and at that time, it was my crowning achievement as a filmmaker.

CHAPTER 10:

My First Shitty Production Gigs

The next six years were a blur. A lot happened, but nothing significant professionally. Through the same network of friends that I met Matt, I met my future wife, Amanda.

In high school, I must have asked out a dozen girls. Every one of them rejected me. It was like Stephen King submitting his work to a Jehovah's Witness Kingdom Hall. It never happened.

So, that awesome experience of falling in love with someone and being totally in the moment never happened for me. Amanda was my first girlfriend, meaning, she didn't go on one date with me and then blow me off in front of her friends.

We couldn't let each other out of our sights. It was a new experience for me, and it took me off-guard, because at this point, at twenty-years-old, I figured I'd never find anyone, and I accepted that.

I had a low opinion of myself. All my friends (*all* meaning Dan and Matt) had girlfriends, and everyone in their social network seemed to have a significant other, too. What was ironic was that, by the time I met Amanda, everyone else became single. Throughout the years, my friends dated a lot of women. Dan was even married, at one point. But Amanda and I were the only ones who stuck together. Six-and-a-half years later, we were married.

But going back to 2003, I had a brand-new girlfriend, so instead of looking for work in the industry and taking any free-lance gig I could find, I spent most of my time hanging out with her. I was desperately trying to catch up on what I missed out on in high school, which was ironic. In high school, I was focused on making my films, because I wasn't distracted. If I did have a girl-friend in high school, my grades would have plummeted.

But here I was, fresh out of film school, hanging around my girlfriend like she was the cure for cancer. And because it was such a new experience, that feeling of finding someone took a long time to wear off.

I remembered feeling insecure and uncomfortable, back when I had a chance to go out with Jessie Cunningham in junior high. I felt that way around a lot of girls, which was the main reason I never dated in high school. I had a few chances to hang out with girls, but I didn't know how to take things to the next step. My pussy internal DNA just wouldn't let me.

For some reason, Amanda felt right. All that nervousness, that being unsure of myself, it went away. Maybe it was because Amanda was an introvert, like me. We met at a mutual friend's house, and when I met her, I had no idea what to say to her. Be-fore I knew it, she was sitting next to me on the couch, talking to me. I have no idea what we even talked about, but I ended up walking her home. The next day, she called me at work and asked if I wanted to hang out again. I wasn't used to a *girl* pursu-ing *me*.

I was still working at Farmer Jack, but the job was as soul-crushing as ever. It never got better. Usually with a new job, you get excited and pumped up the first few weeks, because you're happy to be making money. Then the reality sinks in, and the "Fuck this place" attitude rears its ugly head. I hated working there from day one, so imagine how much worse I felt two years later.

I wasn't finding a lot of work in film production. My dad had a friend who worked for a public access network, which shot high school graduations and volleyball games. It was a paying gig, so I decided to give it a try for a couple days out of the week, when I wasn't scheduled at Farmer Jack-Off.

Initially, we shot a lot of things in the studio. I learned how to work the television cameras, and on occasion I wore a headset, where I listened in to a program director as he told me to grab a shot before locking my camera down for broadcast. He would then give direction to the other two camera operators, switching between the three of us as we recorded a live interview, usually a doctor or local author.

The last time I worked for them was when I worked a gig out in the field. I was a set PA, basically a runner who would run between all the different departments to make sure everything was ready to go. It was a live high school volleyball game, and I was going to assist the director with some of the pre-game interviews. The director resembled Steven Spielberg. He was an older guy who had this over-confidence about him. He was the kind of guy you tried not to piss off.

I had a simple direction: I was to cue the talent off-camera, so they knew when it was time to start saying their lines. It was a simple thing: I was to hold up five fingers, and slowly count down to one. On one, I wasn't supposed to say the number, just count down to the last digit with my finger, then leave the frame. Remember that scene from *Wayne's World*?

Except every time I got down to one and they were ready for the talent to begin, the director yelled, "Cut!" and proceeded to yell at me. "Hey, new guy, what the hell you doing? Let's start over." Again, I did the count down. And each time, the director cut and started yelling at me. The talent looked at me like I was a complete idiot. Finally, one of the other set PA's stepped in and told me, "Look, just let me do it. You're going to keep getting yelled at."

He proceeded to count down, like I had, and the talent was finally able to get through their lines. Afterwards, the director told me he had no idea what they taught at the school I attended, but that I was better off just going home instead of wasting his time.

I was fine with not getting paid the fifty bucks. But here's the funny thing: to this day, I have no idea what I was doing wrong. No one took me aside and explained it to me. My guess, if I had to venture an opinion, was that my fingers were in the frame. But if that was the case, the asshole behind the camera should have told me to reposition my fingers. When we slate a scene, often the camera operator will have to guide us where to put the slate so that it's properly in frame. After that, I decided I was done with public access. Hell, even at Farmer Jack, a job that I absolutely despised, the employees took the time to train me on a cash register. And I didn't have to spend ten-grand at a fancy school for the lessons, either.

Then I worked a freelance gig as a production assistant on the pilot of an up-and-coming TV show. The film *8 Mile* just came out, the loosely-based biopic about Eminem. If you're from Michigan, this film was an especially big deal, and it seemed like everyone was trying to capitalize on it. I'm not sure if the show ever got picked up, but it featured a bunch of local rap artists battling against one another. It wasn't my cup of tea, but it was a paid gig and it seemed more exciting than shooting high school sports.

As it turned out, my role was even more degrading than my public access gig. For whatever reason, they were shooting this thing in the middle of Detroit, in the center of a junkyard. I'm not kidding. All day long, cars drove in and out, kicking up dust. They couldn't have found some low-rent nightclub?

It rained during the day, so my job was to sweep all the water away from the extras using a push broom, as they sat waiting for the rappers to perform. Every extra yelled at me because I swept water in their direction. Who the hell heard of sweeping water in a filthy junkyard? What kind of job was that? I'm damn skippy there is no job title out there that has that in its job description.

The producer, who was my point of contact throughout the day, treated me like an idiot. She talked down to me, getting snippy for no reason. She acted like I was a retard.

I worked from ten that morning until eleven at night, which is a typical day in the film industry. I was paid a hundred bucks, and it was one of the most miserable experiences I ever had on a film set, or any other production. I would have worked later, but at that time, I was bumped over to the night crew at Farmer Jack. I was already going on no sleep, because I got the notice for the job minutes after I'd walked in the door from doing an eight-hour graveyard shift. Now I had to head back to Farmer Jack for another. I was walking from one pile of shit to another.

The producer had the nerve to ask me, "Where do you think you're going?"

"I have to work at my other job."

"Where do you work, a funeral home?" she joked. No, I work a real job making real money, and they don't treat me that much better, but at least I'm not out in the rain taking shit for sweeping muddy water toward a bunch of extras.

I was also working part-time at Toys-R-Us. It might seem like I was trying to kill myself, but there were occasions where Farmer Jack cut back on hours, and the only way I'd be able to pay down my skyrocketing credit card bills was to work a second job. This made it nearly impossible to work night crew, because Toys-R-Us wouldn't let us leave until we had the store back in pristine condition. They didn't have a night crew to do that for them. So, I was late to Farmer Jack almost every night, to the point where I almost got fired. My manager gave me an ultimatum: Toys-R-Us or Farmer Jack. Farmer Jack paid me more, so I had to quit working for Geoffrey the Giraffe. He was an asshole, anyways.

My dad was having the floors done at our house, and the guy doing the work expressed that he was looking for a helper to reduce the workload for his crew. My dad saw how much I was struggling, and wanted to see me make some real money. So, he kind of volunteered me to be this guy's new helper.

Thus, I began a thankless career as a carpet installer.

These guys worked six days a week, and they took the crappiest jobs that no one else wanted. Either small, cramped basements with no heat, or houses that were full of stairs and poles to work around.

They all dropped out of high school, and they all smoked pot. We didn't exactly click. I'm no stranger to work, but manual labor wasn't my calling. It was physically punishing on my knees and back, and with any trade, there's a learning curve. It was a steeper curve for me, because I rarely used tools, and I had a hard time figuring out exactly what it was I was supposed to do. Since my employers were self-employed, they got away with treating me any way they wanted: which was poorly.

At first, they laughed at me when I couldn't figure out how to staple down padding or when I kept smacking myself with the rough side of the carpeting. But after a few weeks, they got nastier. They called me an idiot, cussed me out, and constantly asked what a guy like me was doing installing carpeting. But they never fired me. Despite everything that was said, they kept me around. And they paid me cash. For a while, it became my full-time job, and Farmer Jack became a weekend gig.

One time, I cut the padding wrong. My bosses saw this and broke out laughing. But I was tired of being laughed at. I was tired of being called an idiot. I graduated from high school with an A average. I made movies. I shot a film on 16mm. I wasn't an idiot. But I couldn't convince these fucking losers otherwise.

I remembered back to that day I worked for the public access station, where the director kept yelling at me for doing *something*, but no one would tell me what that *something* was. All that frustration, and no one taught me the *right* way.

Enough was enough. I looked at them and asked, "Why don't you just show me the right way?"

The laughter stopped right there. They looked at each other like I just told them a unicorn was fucking a squirrel. "You're right," one of them said. "All joking aside, we should be showing you the right way."

I'm not saying the job got easier. I continued to take shit

from them for another year before I moved on. But it got a little more tolerable. Sometimes, all it takes is for someone to speak up. A little self-confidence can go a long way.

The next film gig came in the form of an unpaid production assistant position on an independent feature film. *This* was exciting. I was tired of doing the PA thing, but the promise of making new contacts and the experience I'd get working on a feature was what prompted me to throw my name into the proverbial job hat.

From my experience on these things, the more glamorous the production, the less you get paid. And the less you get paid, it seems the less they need you, as if they bring you on strictly as a favor to *you*. Of course, that's not the case. Production assistants do all the running around that the important crew members – the department heads working on *producing* the film – don't want to do. Higher-ups rarely admit it, but production assistants are the backbone of a production, even more so because they're rarely paid. However, because they perform most of the menial tasks, they are generally looked down on.

Years down the road, I would PA on corporate productions, videos that had high production quality, but would typically be shown internally, to company execs or employees. There's little glamour on those types of productions. They aren't the most cinematic projects, but the crew tends to be more down-to-earth because they aren't pretending to be from Hollywood. And honestly, the pay for one of those gigs is pretty damn good.

Switch back to the film set, and I found myself getting talked down to while performing the most basic of tasks, usually for no pay. Experience is great, but it doesn't pay the bills. Most of the time, the tasks I did as a PA were what I could get paid to do at a shitty retail job. Taping down extension cords? I'm sure Home Depot has a job description like that. Washing a dirty storefront window so it's more filmable? On a film set, not only would I *not* get paid for doing it, but some asshole with a megaphone told me I was using the wrong chemicals, or that I was leaving streaks. People who worked in the deli at Farmer Jack got paid nine bucks an hour to clean their windows. I guess having a camera pointed at you really makes a dent in your pay-check.

With this production, I articulated a little more. In be-tween setups, I talked to people in various departments. I asked about the types of cameras they were using, the editing soft-ware they were using, the lighting, the background of the pro-ject, which I knew nothing about when they hired me. Again, I was working two jobs, so I could only make myself available on certain days. But on the days I showed up, I stayed the full twelve hours, and I did whatever I could to help. It wasn't exotic stuff, but I tried to act professionally and did whatever they asked. I even talked shop with the other crew members. Some of them were impressed that I had the opportunity to shoot on film, which most of them never had the chance to do.

I only worked on the production a total of five days, but I was given some important tasks. They needed someone to drive the production truck to another location, because the original driver went home, and no one felt comfortable enough to drive this big cube van. I volunteered, and it was fine. On one occa-sion, I went to get craft services for the crew, and I was even given the task of driving to the airport to pick up one of the leads, who was flying in from India (the film was being financed by a group of Indian investors).

Of course, there were times where it wasn't all sunshine and roses. On two separate occasions, I had food ripped out of my hands. I guess on film sets, no one is required to be polite. Since when is it ever okay to grab something out of someone's hands? I'll give you the scenarios, and then you can decide if this type of behavior was warranted.

I'm not perfect. I make my share of mistakes, and I admit them when I do. See, here I am, admitting that I could have been in the wrong. But the way these offenses were dealt with were completely shitty. They were inappropriate.

First offense: I took a snack from a craft service table that actually *wasn't* there for craft service. It was being used as a set piece for the scene being filmed, which was set in a cafeteria. But there were no signs saying, "Do not touch – this is part of the set." And there were *actual* snacks on display. As soon as I picked up a granola bar, one of the other production assistants came up to me, grabbed the snack from my hands, slammed it down on the table, and *then* explained to me what was going on.

What was so hard about, "Hey, just to let you know, this table is just for the scene we're shooting. I'll put up some signs. Could you just let everyone else know?" I was wrong for not asking. Craft service tables are available at most productions, even low-budget films, so I didn't think anything of it. But grabbing a granola bar from my hand like I was seven-years-old? Why was that appropriate?

The second time this happened was also a food-related offense. Someone brought in a nice heated breakfast for the crew. There was a plethora of Styrofoam containers complete with scrambled eggs, hash browns and sausage links. Without skipping a beat, I picked up one of the containers and started eating. Another production assistant came up to me and grabbed the container from my hands. Seriously?

These were decent sized containers. How was I supposed to know that one container was supposed to be split between several people? Again, no communication, no signs, nothing. And I felt doubly embarrassed, because this was in front of the entire crew. I'm a big guy, slightly overweight, but I also typically don't eat breakfast, which explains my appetite. Eggs, hash browns and sausage on a cold, winter morning? Pretty sexy.

"Hey, I didn't want to embarrass you, but we only have enough so that one container is for several people. Can you share that with some of the other crew members?" There's absolutely nothing wrong with that statement, especially if she would have taken me aside instead of grabbing my breakfast away from me in front of half the crew.

To this day, whenever I'm on a production of any kind and they bring in lunch, I either bring my own from home, or

I ask. And here's how I know I was right in that last situation: whenever I ask, "Hey, is that box for me?", the producer looks at me like I'm insane. "Of course, it's for you. No, we're going to split one box of food between eight people." That last part, of course, is them being sarcastic, but they can't fathom why I'd ask such a weird question. It just beats being completely embarrassed in front of a room full of people just because your stomach's rumbling. For fuck sakes, it wasn't like I was being paid. Feed my ass!

That was an example of a production in which good things and bad things occurred. They were all learning experiences, but the negatives tended to outweigh the positives. Those are the things that stick with us. They help us to grow, but they are never pleasant.

Working on that set made me realize a couple of things, especially a year down the road, when I was struggling to find film work. First, I wasn't good at networking. I talked to crew members, and I even exchanged business cards with a few of them. But I never followed up, and I never made it clear what kind of production work I was good at. When you network, you need to make an impression, so that the people you're hoping will reach out to you remember you. I drove a production van and picked up a cast member from the airport. That's swell, but anyone could have done that. Granted, at that time, I was still learning. I wasn't confident in my abilities. I hadn't even started editing yet. Editing software was still expensive.

I also started to resent how I was treated on the set. I felt (and continue to feel, on a certain level) that people who work on a film production think they're privileged because they're working on a film. They don't even have to be major Hollywood films. My experiences were on local productions. I've worked on productions where the producer stands in front of the entire crew and voices her concerns about getting the film finished because she doesn't want to work a regular 9-5 job.

Working sucks. For 99% of the free world, that's a reality. Imagine how most of us standing there, the ones not being paid, performing all the grunt work that had nothing to do with the creative aspects of the film, the ones working on our days off, felt after hearing that. Here we were, a group of mostly grown adults, being put in our place by a producer who couldn't even get a real job out in L.A. Maybe that wasn't her intention, but I felt completely degraded by that point. Why do artists feel that they don't have to go out and find real work?

That may be why, for the past eighteen years, ever since I graduated high school, I've been working steady, everyday jobs rather than pursuing filmmaking as a viable career. I'm a real person. I'm a man, with a wife, kids, the house in suburbia. I live in the real world. There's no time for fantasizing in my world. A man's got to eat. And when you have mouths to feed, the reality sets in fast, and I can't support a family on experience. I can't pay bills with a permission slip that grants me access to a film set, all so I can talk with other crew members, hoping by some miracle they remember me and invite me to work with them on a paying gig.

But people *do* make careers out of filmmaking. It can be done.

If you're one of those lucky individuals who've been blessed with a career that you absolutely love, that's fantastic. But you should embrace it, and understand how lucky you are. And you need to appreciate the people who've helped you get there. Production assistants might be plentiful, and maybe they tend to get in the way. But most of the time, from my limited experience, they aren't getting paid. Over the years, the title "production assistant" has been further depreciated to a less-favorable title: an intern. It was changed because it gave film-makers a justifiable reason to not pay the help. "He's an intern, he's only here for the experience." Maybe the production assist-ants should be the highest-paid crew members on a production. We're the ones doing the work. We get coffee for the director, wipe stains from windows, tape down extension cords, retrieve actors from the airport, handle craft services, coordinate com-munications between all the departments, answer your phones, act as security guards in order to keep people from accidentally walking into *their own fucking boardroom* because you're in the middle of grabbing a shot. We spray paint your props, we get ignored by the talent, we're rarely taken seriously when we talk about breaking into the industry. And we rarely ever make a dime. Production assistants are needed on the set more than anyone knows or admits.

What would happen if they eliminated production assistants altogether? You think the director's going to make her own fucking coffee? She can't even run a camera. That's why she hired a camera crew and a cinematographer. She gets paid the big bucks to sit in a chair with her last name stenciled on the back, so she can yell, "Lights, camera, action, you fucking assholes."

I'm oversimplifying the director's role. It's been my lifelong ambition to direct a feature-film. And I know people who've made long-lasting relationships on film sets, and have gone on to collaborate on lots of things. But unfortunately, I don't have a lot of those experiences. Like in high school, I have a really hard time forging those important relationships.

If you've ever eaten at a Chinese restaurant, sometimes the menus have information about what type of animal you are, based on the year of your birth. It will tell you the name of the animal, plus the character traits that define said animal. I was born in 1983, the year of the boar. The description of the boar is that he will make few, but long-lasting friends. And that's been true, for the most part. To this day, I still talk with Matt and Dan. And I've been with Amanda for eighteen years, my closest friend, married for eleven of those years. So, I do have the capacity to make friends. It *is* possible. I just haven't found the right production.

I always wondered if things would change if I moved to the big production arenas, New York, L.A., and currently, Atlanta. I wonder if the people are nicer on the bigger crews. Somehow, I doubt it, but maybe people in Michigan are just pretentious. Maybe they have this idea of what real Hollywood people are like, and they try to flaunt it. I'll never forget that producer who declared she didn't want to work a real job. And there's nothing wrong with not wanting to a work a shitty retail job. I've worked plenty of them, and I never found one I liked. But most of us who work on film productions, especially as "interns", *have* to work those kinds of jobs when we're not being paid. So, maybe as a producer, your job should be to show compassion for those people who are helping you out and not getting paid. After all, what happens if you fire one of us? Nothing. Half of nothing is still nothing. What are you going to say to us, once you've terminated our employment? "You'll never work for free in this town again."

Working on a film should not be stressful. It's art. As a filmmaker, you're demonstrating your passion for a story you want to tell. It's not that far removed from painting, creating a sculpture, or writing a novel. There are a lot more people involved, all invested in getting your vision realized. You need to have respect for that. If you want to treat someone like shit, go take away food from your D.P., or your cinematographer, or your script supervisor. After all, they're the ones being paid to fuck shit up. If *I* make a clumsy mistake, so what? You get what you pay for. After all, you *are* paying me in experience, so I'd say a few missteps are just par for the course.

In 2006, I quit my stint as a carpet installer's bitch and decided to focus on achieving full-time status at Farmer Jack. My goal was to get into a mid-management position, work a normal nine-to-five shift, and then spend my evenings focusing on making my own movies. I was no longer interested in working for free on someone else's film. If things were going to happen, I needed to make them happen.

Eventually, I was promoted to a full-time customer service manager. I was guaranteed full-time hours, and I was done every day by five, which was my goal. I transferred to Walled Lake, which was a bit of a commute, but it was far more laid back. I really liked my employees, and my supervisors were alright, too. Hell, on my birthday, a couple of my employees bought me a cake. They sang "Happy Birthday" to me in the breakroom. That was the only time that happened, at any job.

Then, in 2007, it was announced that Farmer Jack was closing its doors. They were going out of business. Farmer Jack had been a popular Michigan grocery store for decades, and now they were calling it quits. The real reasoning behind it is stupid, drawn-out, and not interesting enough for me to talk about, but I worked there for seven years. All of a sudden, for the first time since high school, I was facing unemployment.

CHAPTER 11:

The Shit I Did Just for Fun

To make matters worse, my parents were on the brink of divorce.

I was in my early twenties, so you'd think that my parents getting divorced shouldn't have been a big deal.

Let me tell you: it's a big deal regardless of where you are in life. No matter how bad it got for them in the end, they're still my parents. For the first time, I felt like I was from a broken family. Jack and Glenn were having a harder time dealing with it. However, Jack was much better at making friends than I was. He was (and still is) extremely personable. He had a girlfriend at that time, so he wasn't home all that much, and tried to pretend everything was fine.

But since I also had Amanda, and I was spending an increasing amount of time at her house, that left Glenn to fend for himself. And when I *was* home, Matt and Dan came over into the late hours of the night, and we'd terrorize the fuck out of him.

Glenn, like me, had a hard time making friends. When Matt and Dan came over, Glenn tried to hang out with us, and we'd try to get him to leave. And when he didn't leave, we picked on him. It got out of hand. Yes, we were assholes to him. I like to think that we were brothers, and we were horsing around. But I know Glenn resents a lot of it. Not only did he have to deal with my parents' continuing insanity, but his dickhead brother and his asshole friends would pick on him. Life really sucked for him.

But on a few occasions, we actually included him in a few things.

Matt, Dan, and I spent a lot of our evenings making videos. Not films, so much; films require planning. Usually, the night started with me taking out my video camera and recording the three of us goofing off. From there, they came up with funny things to do on-camera, and this is when I started putting my editing skills to the test.

I took these random clips of us goofing off, and I edited chunks of them in a specific order. Sometimes I sped them up, other times I slowed them down, or played them in reverse. I put on a goofy filter, added sound effects; the bottom line was, what turned into a minor annoyance for Dan and Matt became a pastime, like friends getting together to play cards on a slow Friday night.

At first, they hated when I broke out the video camera, because they didn't know why I was taping all the time. And I taped *all the time*. I never left the house without my camera, because I wanted to improve on my camera skills, and you'd be surprised what kind of shit you can find just by cruising a major stretch of highway.

But once I took that footage and edited it together in a condensed format, they got a kick out of it. That led to us making these little impromptu films.

The one that stood out was *Detroit Vice*. Dan was a huge *Miami Vice* fan, so he had this idea for a parody, where he and Matt were Detroit cops who went out to bust Mexican drug dealers.

And Glenn played the Mexican drug dealer.

The film starts with Matt and Dan, as Sonny Burnett and Rocko Rodriguez, driving through the streets of Detroit (my little suburban side-street), talking about a sexual encounter Dan had the night before. The first line of dialogue is Dan saying, "So,

I fucked that chick last night."

It was liberating, because for the first time since *Star Whores*, I wasn't making it for anyone but me, so I didn't have to concern myself with censorship.

After Dan's graphic sex story (which involves teeth and a pearl necklace – use your imagination), they notice a shady character pedaling drugs by a street corner (the parking lot of a daycare center).

They pull over, get out of the car and interrogate Glenn. Dan has a PlayStation light gun as his weapon of choice (you can see the cable dangling from it). As they begin frisking Glenn, Glenn freaks out and starts to run. Dan and Matt give chase, and gunshots are fired. At this point, Dan has Glenn on the ground, but something interesting happened to Matt. Matt was wearing these button-down pants that snap up along the sides. While he ran, somehow his pants came unbuttoned and before he knew it, his pants were down around his ankles. While this happened, he never broke character. You hear him saying, "I'll get him, Sonny!" In the distance, Dan's looking off at Matt, screaming, "What the fuck are you doing?"

Matt finally rejoins with Sonny, who asks Glenn, "Do you have any drugs on you?" Glenn just keeps repeating, "Yo mama!" As they pat him down and get him to his feet, Glenn screams, "Rape! Rape!" Glenn was part of the early generation of online gamers, and his big thing was "Rape!" He screamed it whenever we fucked with him. As Matt and Dan manhandle him into their "squad car" (my beat-up Prism), Glenn shouts, "Stop raping me up the ass, you racist gringo!" Dan couldn't stop cracking up on-camera.

The film wraps with Dan saying to Matt, "Let's go get some more of those Detroit hookers." As they get into the car, Dan looks into the camera and says, "Another day in Detroit." As they drive off, Matt shouts, "Pussy!" And then we go to credits.

We had such a fun time making that video. I edited the project that night, Dan and Matt looking over my shoulder the whole time. They were fascinated with how quickly I put it together. Dan gave me ideas on how to animate the titles, and with the added sound effects, it made the film shine.

With a growing collection of goofy videos, I started a YouTube channel. This was a weird time for content creators, because YouTube started this trend of introducing *shows* on the internet. A viral video used to be someone's cat doing something remotely funny, or someone pulling a well-timed prank on a friend; the kind of short, thirty-second clips you can now find on Instagram. But the more I traversed this strange new website, I realized that people were starting to put in more effort into what they were uploading. There were series, complete with graphics, title cards, and full-blown editing. YouTube was a game changer in how people viewed content.

◆ ◆ ◆

2007 was a depressing year for me. It was also a big year of personal change. Aside from my parents splitting up, my dad's waning health, and the loss of my job, I was given the option to go back to college. Michigan's governor was implementing a program called No Worker Left Behind. Targeted at people who were laid off and struggling to re-enter the work force, Michigan paid qualifying candidates up to $10,000 to go back to school and get a degree. The catch was, it had to be a program that showed potential for growth in Michigan. Michigan isn't a great state to find work in to begin with, unless you work for one of the big three auto companies, but we were in the middle of a recession. Even the auto companies suffered.

I was one of the first candidates. I continued seeking work at Michigan Works, a government-sanctioned employment agency, which also acted as my access point into the program, provided I jump through several hoops.

There were two things I ever dreamed of being: a writer and a filmmaker. To most people, those are unusually high goals, maybe even a bit unrealistic. I'm not saying that I was too good to work a typical nine-to-five; I'm just pointing out that those are the only things I had interest pursuing. It's like when someone asks you what your dream car is. It doesn't matter if you're going to be able to afford it; we can all dream, can't we?

Through the wonderful world of computer emulators, I was slowly getting back into gaming, something I hadn't indulged in since high school. If you noticed, I spoke highly about video games at the beginning of the book, but that quickly faded off, didn't it? I also wrote more, and I edited videos frequently. I wasn't a computer whiz, but I knew my way around a computer.

Amanda's brother-in-law made a killing working as a computer technician. We talked a few times about its potential. He lived in Florida, so the job market was different, but computers was considered a "high-growth market" in Michigan. So, I bit the bullet, decided to try my hand at the whacky world of computer science, and enrolled at Oakland Community College, where I pursued my Associates.

I've gone to college a total of seven years, and I've always loved the academic atmosphere; and no, I'm not being sarcastic. Maybe it was because I was slightly older than most of the other students. I was in my early-to-mid-twenties when a lot of these kids were fresh out of high school. Because my tuition costs depended on getting good grades, I pushed myself harder than I ever had in grade school.

When I first enrolled, I freaked out about taking a math class, because math wasn't one of my strong suits. After barely passing my first exam, the professor told me I should consider enrolling in a more entry-level class. Michigan Works only had so much money they could give me, and if I took any classes outside of my projected budget, I'd have to pay for them out-of-pocket. So, I studied every night. Math is great in that, it's something you can practice. There *are* right and wrong answers. If I didn't understand how to work out a problem, I went to the back of the book and sought out the correct answer. It sounds like cheating, but by knowing the answer, I worked out the problem until I arrived at the proper conclusion. Like anything else, once you repeat the process, it starts to sink in. In the words of the great Morgan Freeman, I started to find brains I never knew I had.

When it came to my computer courses, this was not a program where we were going to learn how to build computers. It was centered around jobs that used computers to complete tasks, which meant a lot of time studying programming, web design, systems analysis, networking, and database development. I excelled at almost every subject. The thing was, no matter how well I did, I couldn't see myself working in a professional capacity. I wasn't passionate about it. Not to mention, when it came to programming and coding, I couldn't get a firm grasp on it, and I struggled with it daily.

◆ ◆ ◆

I also got hired in at Bullseye's, a horrible company to work for, and I was miserable every day I walked through those doors. I didn't jive with a lot of the employees, at first. This changed as time went on, and they saw how much we had in common. I worked in electronics, so we were mainly a group of people who played video games and watched movies.

The biggest problem with Bullseye's were the team leaders. Most of them didn't know how to run a team, let alone talk to people.

My direct supervisor was this aggressive, militant meathead named Michael. He was young, about my age, and he walked like he had a stick up his ass. He was always in a hurry to get somewhere.

From my first day, I knew he didn't like me. There was something about me that made him want to tag me like a shark, and I ended up in his office every other day. I wasn't meeting the requirements of the job. How the fuck hard is it to stock shelves, ring up customers, and bullshit about TVs and video games?

◆ ◆ ◆

Despite my suck-ass new retail job, I continued to make videos on a weekly basis. I indulged in my passion for films by producing movie reviews. In October, I started my own annual horror-a-thon, which I dubbed *31 Days of Slashers; 31 DOS* for short. With these videos, I always produced them at the last minute. Sometimes I wrote, recorded, and edited a video once a day so I made sure I had at least one review ready to go for each day in October.

With my YouTube channel, I never found a good way to promote my content. Even after flooding my description with the appropriate tags, most of my videos never seemed to get many views. On occasion I got lucky, and timing was part of it. For example, my horror reviews were more popular around Halloween. When *Star Wars: The Force Awakens* was about to be released to Blu-ray, I did a lengthy review of the film just days before its release date, which netted a decent 4,000 views.

If you search YouTube for movie reviews, you'll discover that *everyone* does them. Everyone has their own format. Usually, it's just a talent sitting in front of the camera discussing the movie in question, but the market is oversaturated with people who either watch movies or stream video games.

But I enjoyed writing and talking about movies, so I kept doing it. Eighty percent of my content revolved around movies. This was where I started to master the art of video editing. Editing a movie review is a straightforward process, but I was churning them out so quickly, that it taught me how to take shortcuts and speed up my turnaround time. Before long, I was creating three- and four-minute videos within a couple of hours, from the time I recorded the voiceover to the time I was ready to export the finished video.

As with everything, there were negatives and positives to these videos. First, the negatives, because those are more fun to talk about.

With videos like *Detroit Vice* being made public, anyone could look at them; including professional production companies looking to hire established editors and videographers.

I didn't think anything of it. After all, people were making a living doing these kinds of videos. But I guess I wasn't there yet. I wasn't making any money for my efforts. It was a fun hobby that allowed me to pursue my interest in filmmaking. But I was also still pursuing legitimate production work.

At this point, I was done taking unpaid, entry-level PA positions on independent films that were only important to the Metro Detroit area. I was looking for more steady work in the corporate arena, working on things like promotional content for local businesses.

One time, I had a phone interview with a hiring manager who was looking for freelance videographers. I didn't know it yet, but he saw *Detroit Vice*; and he challenged me on it.

At first, his questions seemed straightforward. He asked about my experience and the kind of work I'd done previously. Then he mentioned *Detroit Vice*. He asked me to explain it. I was honest with him. I told him it was a video I'd done with friends, and we tried to make it funny, but it was targeted for a more film-oriented crowd. He proceeded to ask if I thought the swearing was necessary, and why I thought I'd be a good candidate if I was making such raunchy videos. Obviously, I didn't get the position.

On the one hand, I thought it was unfair. I did a ton of videos that were perfectly normal and non-offensive. He just happened to see one of the few films that *was* offensive, and that's what he used to pass judgment on me. I guess if a filmmaker makes R-rated movies, they're incapable of filming high-end commercials. That was my takeaway from this guy.

On the other hand, I started to question the types of videos I put out there. I didn't feel this was fair because most of the online personalities I watched didn't refrain from swearing. For a while, I started taking down the videos that Matt, Dan, and I worked on, because I didn't want them to hurt my career *before* I got a career.

On the positive side, with all the experience I had editing, I started to get a small trickle of freelance editing jobs. I started to build a reputation as a fast editor, and filmmakers were looking for someone who could do same-day edits.

MPI, little did I know, was asked to run a small filmmaking workshop in Frankenmuth, which held an annual event dubbed the Made-in-Michigan Film Festival. The festival ran for three days and was held at Frankenmuth High School, where Michigan filmmakers with little-to-no exposure could have their films shown.

The filmmaking workshop was held on a Saturday, typically the busiest day of a film festival. High school kids signed up, showed up to the cafeteria at eight in the morning, and started brainstorming ideas for a short film. Then, they had six hours (!) to write, direct, and edit their film before it was shown that same day at the festival.

The workshop was run by Lindy, a former graduate of MPI who attended years after I attended the program. She put out a feeler for same-day editors, and naturally, I applied. And I got the job.

I've talked a lot about my negative experiences in the film industry, and I have my own reasons why I don't actively pursue the industry as much as I probably should.

But working with Lindy was one of the best experiences I've ever had in the industry. It was a lot of fun, and it was a paying gig. Lindy, Joe, another MPI graduate, and I showed up early in the morning to get set up. Lindy was the de facto producer who ran the brainstorming session and got the kids hyped to shoot whatever movie they conjured up. Joe did all the technical production stuff; running camera, setting up lights, and recording audio. He formed a little production crew composed of the students, and would rotate out directors, so anyone who wanted to try their hand at directing got their shot.

My job was to help in any capacity I could, until they

finished filming their first completed scene. At that point, Joe handed me the memory card, where I'd dump the footage to my laptop, hand the card back to Joe, and begin editing as the kids continued to make their movie.

It was an intense experience. As soon as I finished up the final key strokes, Joe handed me back the card, which contained even more shots. I was under constant pressure to get this thing done, and without a proper script, sometimes I'd have to guess the correct order of the shots.

With an hour left to go before we had to hand in the final film, I'd sit around with the kids and show them the rough cut, letting them make any changes they saw fit, all the while explaining what I was doing, or how I might choose to make a specific editing decision. It was a blast.

In all the years I edited for the workshop, it was always hectic, always a creative joy; but sometimes, it proved to be a colossal, technical pain in the ass.

The editor needs to be a total neat freak when it comes to their job, but they also need to know their equipment.

Backing up my footage is always priority number one. The last thing I want to have happen is to have the camera operator delete a memory card *before* I copy over the files. I always bring an external hard drive, one of those little canvas drives that fits easily into a backpack or pant pocket, and when I transfer over files from a card, I always make sure I have two sets; one on my internal hard drive, and one on my external drive. You can never have too many backups.

My first year working for the film workshop was mostly great; until the last hour, where my computer froze, and I was unable to re-open the project file I'd been working on the whole morning. See, while I backup my video files, I never thought to make duplicate copies of my *project* files. And to make matters worse, it was completely my fault.

The kids decided to make a horror movie, so naturally, I chose this creepy font for the opening titles. However, the font I used was graphics-intensive, and my PC just couldn't handle it.

And before you yell out, "That's what you get for editing on a PC instead of a Mac," this could have easily happened on a MacBook Pro.

Fortunately, Lindy reminded me that Adobe Premiere auto-saves your work. Somewhere on my drive, there was an earlier version of the project. The question was, how far back would I have to go? If the only auto-save was while editing my first scene, I'd be screwed. I'm fast, but there's no way I'm editing an entire film in an hour.

I got lucky. I lost a few of my edits, but most of my work was backed up. As I changed my awesome, scary font to Times New Roman, exported the project and burned it to DVD, Lindy raced down the hall to the auditorium so she could tell the showrunners that we were on our way. Joe and I raced each other down the hall a minute later, laughing our asses off. Somehow, we'd pulled it off; an entire short film in six hours.

The following day, while I was at home, I went back and made some finishing touches, putting in the proper titles, adding visual effects and additional sounds to enhance it. Lindy and Joe really appreciated the extra work I put in, and for the next three years, I went back and served as their editor. It was a no-brainer.

Thanks to Joe, I also got to edit a project he and his friend, Ed, worked on. A radio station, 89X, was hosting an 89-Hour Film Festival, similar to the 48 Hour Film Project. If you're not familiar with how the 48 Hour Film Project works, essentially teams of filmmakers get together and are given a pre-determined theme and tagline, which they must employ in their film. Then they have 48 hours to make their film before turning it in to the judges. This was a longer version of that.

Ed shot all his footage, and he had sixteen hours before he had to submit the film; and he had no editor. Joe contacted me and asked if I'd be willing to help. The payment would be a steak dinner and all the Mountain Dew I could drink. The best part about the job was that I'd only have to drive a few blocks to the location.

From four in the afternoon until five the following morning, I edited Ed's film. The hardest part was, like with most professional productions, the sound was recorded separately from the picture. Usually it's not a big deal – any editor worth his or her salt can sync sound to picture without a second thought. But on such a tight time crunch, it added another level of stress.

By midnight, I had a rough cut ready to go. The rest of the time was spent making tweaks. I did at least eight revisions before Ed locked it down for final cut.

That night, the films were shown at the Emagine Theater in Royal Oak. The radio station had an awesome red-carpet ceremony; a little pretentious, but hell, it was the closest I'd ever felt to being a movie star. I even had my picture taken with the crew.

Out of the eleven films that were shown, we didn't win for best short film, but we were one of the three runners-up, which still felt damn good. It was one of the best gigs I ever had.

CHAPTER 12:

A Walk Beside Eden, Loose Change,
and the Bull@$%* in Between

Meanwhile, back at Bullseye's, every day was a slog. I no longer enjoyed working in electronics, because the customers I dealt with didn't believe anything I said. They asked me a question, I'd answer it as honestly as I could, and they'd tell me I was lying.

One guy, an older fuck, asked what he needed to get such a vibrant picture on his high-definition television. He saw all the displays on the back wall and swore that his television wasn't displaying as sharp of a picture. I told him all he needed was an HDMI cable. You know what he said?

"I don't believe you. I think I'll do a little more research on that."

Another time this rich, snooty woman wanted to know what an ISO was on a digital camera. Essentially, the ISO controls the iris on the camera lens, regulating the amount of light that enters the frame.

The lady responded by saying, "You're lying to me. I know you're lying." Then why even ask the fucking question if you already knew the answer, you snooty rich cunt? It would have been worth getting fired just so I could have said that.

I was on the verge of moving in with Amanda and her

mom, who lived on the other side of town. I put in for a transfer to another store, and one of my managers asked what it would take to get me to stay.

I couldn't remember making so little money. Even Farmer Jack hired me in at a rate that surpassed minimum wage. If I was going to work at that location, I'd be commuting from Amanda's house. So, I told my manager exactly what I'd need: a two-dollar-an-hour raise. She laughed and said, "Yeah, you're not getting that."

If I *had* gotten that raise, I would be making as much as an entry-level team lead, as I was bound to discover two years later.

The transfer went through, and before I knew it, I was finally out of my dad's house and on my own. At that point, Amanda and her mom moved to a nice little trailer park, and Amanda's mom, who was in her mid-sixties, was getting ready to move to Florida. Amanda wasn't working, so if I didn't move in with her, she would have been forced to move out of state. So, I moved in, started paying the lot rent, and as soon as her mom was settled in at her daughter's house in Port St. Lucie, she sent us a little extra money to help us out.

The stress quickly started to mount. I barely made enough to make lot rent, let alone to buy food and pay other bills. I was almost done with college, but I wasn't having luck finding any IT jobs. I secured a couple of internships, both paid positions, but they didn't last long.

The first internship was something I was able to do from home, and it was updating databases remotely from my computer. I logged in to the company's database and ran a few simple commands that automated a process, in turn updating the databases from their end. It was a simple job, I only did it for two hours a day, and because it was a mostly automated task, I wasn't learning anything. My boss was a nice guy, but after a while, he forgot I worked for him. Eventually, the process only took about twenty minutes a day, so I ended up quitting.

The second internship was yet another frustrating experience, and was the sole reason I decided not to pursue IT. The job involved installing VoIP (voice over IP) phones for big companies, phones that ran over an internet connection. The guy who hired me also ran the business, and he expected me to be more knowledgeable than I was.

When it comes to computers, or hell, most electronics, sometimes the only way to know if something works is by trial and error. I don't claim to understand how everything works; sometimes, I just plug something in, and hopefully, I'll see the little blue light pop on.

I approached this job the same way. I took a basic networking course, but with no real-world experience, a lot of the concepts went over my head. When I needed to troubleshoot a specific problem, my boss got frustrated if I couldn't figure out a solution on the spot. Rather than think about how a network works, I started plugging in cables to see what worked and what didn't. This aggravated him to no end. While most of the job was paid, he didn't believe in paying for training, since I was in college and supposedly getting my training from there. I never heard of such a backwards philosophy. Most jobs pay for your training.

I even got into a screaming match with the guy. He gave me my own personal VoIP phone to use at home, strictly for business purposes, of course. I spent ten hours trying to configure it, and every time I called him with a question, he got more agitated with me. He couldn't understand how it was taking me so long to figure out a simple thing like configuring a phone.

By now, you should see a pattern. Regardless of whether it's assisting with a film production, installing carpet, or configuring a computer network, it takes me a little extra time to comprehend everything *and* gain the confidence needed to do a good job.

In school, I had an entire semester to get good at something. I went home for hours and studied my ass off, and if I struggled with something, I kept at it until I came up with the right solution. I got the grades because I had a strong work ethic, not because I was born with book smarts. I've always had to work hard at the things I'm good at. I don't believe anyone is born talented. We have certain passions, we follow those passions, and if we work hard enough at them, we eventually get good at them.

But when you're forced to do something that you have no passion for, that's a challenge; and there are a lot of people who don't have the patience for that. I began to see the catch-22 of the computer business. Companies were looking to hire eighteen-year-olds with thirty years of experience. That's not limited to the computer industry, but given how fast technology changes, the younger generation is always going to have the upper-hand in that field.

The bottom line: I liked the work I was doing in school, but the jobs I found weren't doing it for me. My brother-in-law told me to stick with it, because the money was great. But I've never been one to pursue something just because of an increased income. We should be able to live out our lives pursuing our passions. Work is just the means to an end. A guy's got to eat.

I was proud to finally have a degree, but once I graduated from the program, I couldn't find any work. So much for all that growth in Michigan. I looked for over a year, and as time passed, I realized that an Associates is useless unless you have a focus in something. I didn't have the money to keep going back to school, so I made a conscious decision to chalk it up as a great learning experience and a nice piece of wall décor. My degree looks great next to my film certificate.

But, as you know, I wanted to be a filmmaker. So, I began working on another film.

◆ ◆ ◆

Between 2002 and 2007, I hadn't *directed* anything. Matt, Dan, and I churned out a ton of videos, but they weren't *films*. They were funny videos created out of boredom.

During our relationship, I realized that Amanda suffered from mild seizures. I only witnessed her having one, but it was scary. I didn't know anything about her condition, only that people typically didn't die from seizures. However, my mind tended to go to dark places. I started to wonder what it would be like if seizures *were* fatal.

Amanda and I were together for four years at that point, and while I hadn't proposed to her yet, I had no immediate plans of cutting her loose. We were still inseparable. Thinking about what life would be like if I faced her imminent death became the basis for my next film.

A Walk Beside Eden was unique in several ways. First, it was my first love story. I didn't want to write a lot of gushy dialogue. As fond as I am of George Lucas and as much time as I spent defending his *Star Wars* prequels, I can't defend the cringe-worthy romantic exchanges between Natalie Portman and Hayden Christensen. To avoid that, I decided to make a silent film.

But most silent films still have dialogue, employing the use of word bubbles or what are known as *intertitles* (those decorative backgrounds with text notifying the audience that someone is talking in the scene). And most silent films are black and white. My film was in color, and I was attempting to tell the story through character emotion and music – no intertitles. It was a strange choice, but I was in the mood to be experimental. Hell, my last film was derivative of a bunch of movies, so I wanted this one to be a more original work.

As with most of my scripts, it started out a little too close to home. I was writing about situations that actually happened, rather than focusing on a fictional narrative. For example, part of the inspiration for the film was a girl I tried to hook up with before I met Amanda. After a year, I finally gave up because I realized I wasn't her type. This happened when all my friends were in relationships, and I was the only one in this social circle who was single. Then Amanda came along, and everything worked out. But I incorporated part of that into my script.

The script was also about the protagonist's inability to

deal with death. Amanda lost a shocking number of friends and family to cancer. On the other hand (and I'm knocking on wood as I say this), I hadn't lost anyone close to me. However, because I spent so much time taking my dad to hospitals and watching his health decline through the years, I always felt that his funeral was right around the corner. I always fretted losing him, but I also knew that he was beyond any sort of cure.

The script told a story that realized all my worst fears. What I wanted to do was show a movie to people and get a reaction from them. I wanted to make people cry. I know it sounds like a cruel ambition, but I enjoy crying at movies. And when it comes to movies, I tend to be very bitch-like.

There were a few hurdles. You would think that my biggest roadblock was budget, but I've proven time and again that you can make a movie with little-to-no money; it just depends on how much you're willing to compromise, and how creative your problem-solving skills are. My biggest obstacle has always been casting. Like I said when I discussed *Attack of the B Movies*, all the good actors want to be paid. And those willing to work for free are typically inexperienced.

That isn't always the case. There are quite a few actors out there who realize that making films can be both difficult and expensive, and they're willing to work for free provided they get a favor down the road. I was able to find a few of these actors for *Eden,* but I had to dig deep.

Then, there were the locations. Finally, after years of being restricted to my parents' house, I was forcing myself to shoot at other venues. The script called for a hospital, a cemetery, a mall, a restaurant, and a beach. By hook or by crook, I was going to find some way to get access to all these places.

And even if, by some miracle all these things fell into place, I was still going to be limited by my equipment. I didn't have any money. I started working on *Eden* while I was between jobs, because it was the first time in a while that I had time to work on something creative. As a birthday gift, my dad bought me my own mini-DV camcorder, which I was eccentric for. For its time, it gave me the best quality footage I ever had. But I was trying to take *A Walk Beside Eden* seriously, and a camcorder was still a consumer-level piece of equipment. There was no way I'd be able to shoot on film or rent a higher-quality camera. So, I was going to try and be more creative with my shots, picking places that had a decent level of natural light so I could get the most out of my video.

The first scene I shot was at Andary's, this little family restaurant that Amanda and her mom frequented. The owner was one of Amanda's former teachers, and he allowed us to use his restaurant provided we ordered a meal and we shot closer to closing time, when business died down.

The scene was an innocent little food fight, to be used during a montage where Adam, the protagonist, was falling in love with Eden, his love interest. Adam was to slowly start antagonizing Eden, until she fought back, and the two begin flinging food at one another. This attracts the attention of the restaurant patrons, including one of the waitresses, who proceeds to kick them out.

As usual, I had to double down and act along with directing. And because Amanda didn't want me kissing a random girl (and because she didn't have to memorize any dialogue), she opted to play the role of Eden. Dan was the camera operator.

We shot the bulk of the scene within a couple of hours, and it went pretty much as planned. Later, as the film got closer to completion, I'd grab a couple of insert shots of people watching the food fight (mostly members of Amanda's family).

There were two scenes I needed in the cemetery: one where Adam's father passes away, and the climactic final scene, where Eden is buried. First, I called around to several local cemeteries, just to see if I could get permission to film in any of them. One of the pastors I talked to recommended we find a walk-in cemetery, one where people can visit all day long and not attract attention from outsiders. We found one such cemetery in Birmingham. I shot both scenes back-to-back, employing the help of my mom, Glenn, and Dan's mom.

As far as props, I couldn't afford to rent a casket, so I had to think about what I was going to show on film. This was my solution: I took two of those big, plastic totes you find at Target, stacked a big, wooden door on top of them, and then placed a sheet over the entire structure. The way the sheet contoured to the door, it looked like a casket that was covered up. It's amazing how much money you can save just by eyeballing a few household items.

My biggest concern was, I was afraid the police might see us filming, stop production and ask to see some sort of permit. But for all they knew, we were just a small funeral procession going about our business. Thankfully, I never saw one cop car.

Originally, there was supposed to be a scene that took place inside of a populated mall. We couldn't get the clearance to shoot there, and even if we did, having all those businesses in the background posed another slew of problems. I rewrote the scene and decided to use only the mall exterior, shooting in the parking lot. That way, we at least got a sense of the location.

We had the same problem with the hospital setting, which was understandable given all the privacy act laws. For this location, I fully expected to be turned away. In the scene, Eden's parents are told about her fatal condition, with a doctor explaining her x-ray. There were also several sequences with Eden in a hospital bed. This was the emotional backbone of the film, so it was integral.

Again, I decided to shoot the scene outside of the hospital. Eden's parents pace back and forth, and I enter the scene holding a bouquet of flowers. Then the doctor enters the fray and explains Eden's unfortunate medical situation. I understood that under real-world circumstances, this would probably happen within a doctor's office. What was important was that I conveyed the message: if the audience understood what was happening, the exact location didn't matter. To further convey we were at a hospital, I grabbed shots of the emergency entrance, signs leading to the entrance, and EMS vehicles coming and going. I even grabbed a shot of us driving up to the hospital, simulating an ambulance arriving on the scene.

For the scenes of Eden in her hospital bed, I dressed Amanda's room to look like a hospital room. This wasn't a huge undertaking. I kept the camera tight on Amanda, making sure I didn't show too much of her room. No matter how hard you try, a bedroom will never look like a hospital room. At that point, Darlene, Amanda's mom, was on oxygen. We used one of her extra oxygen hoses to make it look like Amanda was in critical condition. Darlene also had one of those bags used for IVs, so we taped it to a tripod. On camera, it looks like one of those IV poles stationed by the side of a hospital bed.

If you pay close enough attention, it's obvious that the whole hospital sequence was stitched together. But with clever editing, a series of random shots strewn together can suddenly create a convincing scene.

Shooting some of these scenes proved to be more emotional than I thought. The hardest thing was, Adam and Eden's relationship obviously carried the film, and neither Amanda nor myself had any acting training. I had to carry the film and try to look disheartened by her passing, which meant I had to cry on film. I give professional actors a lot of credit, because being in a constant emotional state is taxing. There's more to it than simply thinking about an upsetting time – you put yourself in a situation when it's not actually happening to you.

During the filming of Eden's funeral scene, I came surprisingly close to tears. For one, Amanda wasn't there when we shot the scene, so the absence of her presence was felt. In fact, aside from Dan, who was still operating the camera, I was in the presence of strangers. I literally just met Jim and Kim, the actors playing Eden's bereaved parents, one day prior to filming with them. At one point, Dan got concerned when he saw tears flowing. Ah, the life of an actor.

There was also a subplot, in which my character tried to get with a girl who wasn't into him. I was able to find an actress suitable for the part, and we shot an entire scene with her. However, one of the drawbacks to shooting with actors who aren't getting paid is that, you can't do much when they leave your production to go work on a project that can afford to pay them. Again, I had to improvise and shuffle around scenes to make up for the lost actress, since I really didn't want to have to reshoot the entire scene. The more I thought about it, the scene should only serve as a prelude to the main story, because anything else would detract from the film. I recalled Shakespeare's *Romeo & Juliet*, in which Romeo originally goes after Rosaline, but instead falls for Juliet. The original script would have had this other female character dating this bully-type, and the bully constantly pushing around my character until I find true love with Eden. It convoluted the story, so the actress's departure was a blessing in disguise.

The other hard scene to film was the death of my dad; or rather, Adam's dad. As I mentioned, my dad's health declined quite a bit over the last few years. It got to the point where he hardly left his bedroom, he almost never wore clothes, and he was forced to digest a healthy dose of pills every day. Obviously, the character was based on my dad, but it also gave me an opportunity to shoot a scene and not have to look for an additional actor. My dad played the part, provided he didn't have to do any acting, which was easy given how sick he really was.

In the scene, my character feeds him dinner, but he overcooks it, causing his dad to choke. In a fit of rage, his dad flings the plate of food at him, forcing his son to clean it up. The scene ends with Adam tucking his father back into bed and leaving the room depressed.

Some people questioned why I felt the need to use my dad as a subject in the film. The central theme was how we deal with death, and since death has always been a morbidly fascinating and altogether depressing subject for me, that was why I approached it as such. Was I supposed to film the scene with a clown juggling act going on in the background? The reality is, sometimes movies are sad. I was aiming to make a sad movie, because 2007 was a sad year for me, and an artist projects himself through his work.

What pushed the scene over the edge was, while my dad was still running his computer business on a limited basis, I asked him to take a photo with me. I would then use the photo during the funeral scene.

To show people that I was working on a film, I edited together my dad's funeral scene as a sort of "trailer" and posted it online. My family went crazy. I had a cousin message me, crying that her Uncle Bernie passed away and no one told her. I guess shame on me for not opening with some sort of warning, but it got the desired effect. The video footage of my dad's "funeral" was effective, and it fooled quite a few people.

Once all the footage was shot and I had a rough cut assembled, the next step was to find music. All throughout filming, I thought about the music that was used for the *Forrest Gump* trailer. The music in that trailer wasn't Alan Silvestri's original score, but it was incredibly sweeping. So, that initial cut of the film used a lot of music from *Forrest Gump*, amongst other composers. None of it was licensed, but in 2007, I knew next to nothing about copyright law. That was the cut I showed people.

I was damn proud of the finished product. Even though it still had a soft video look, and it had the smallest crew imaginable – namely, Dan and myself – it was the most ambitious film I ever worked on, even more so than *Attack of the B Movies*. The scope of the work was broader, with all the locations and the emotionally potent kind of storytelling I was going for. It was thirty-five minutes long, and it told a moving story.

My parents were the first ones I showed it to. They were impressed. It looked like a *film*. With *Attack of the B Movies*, they couldn't relate to it because they didn't watch a lot of movies; much less, the kinds of movies I referenced. But this was the kind of story my mom could really get into, and of course, because Amanda was considered family at that point, seeing the end scene in the cemetery pushed her to tears.

I got the same result from my grandparents, who had nothing but nice things to say about it; and I trusted them, because they were always honest with me. Years back, I showed my grandpa *Oedipus the King*, and he didn't understand it. But here, he fully grasped the story. At this screening, Amanda was with me, so by the time the credits rolled, my grandma was balling. She immediately got up from her couch and gave Amanda a hug.

But it was understandable that my family would react this way. They knew Amanda, and the film made it feel like she passed away. I wondered how the film would play for an audience who wasn't connected with the cast.

I submitted the film to a local film festival. The film was rejected on the grounds that it was too long, and they couldn't ask their audience to sit through a thirty-minute silent film.

I'll give them the length requirements. Thirty minutes is a bit long for most of these film festivals, when the average length is five-to-ten minutes. But asking their audience to sit through a silent film? The only reason they were able to run a film festival at all was because decades ago, a bunch of theater owners got together and tried their hand at feature storytelling. And at that time, *all* movies were silent. I get that silent films are from another era, but four years later, we got *The Artist*, a truly great film that's all about the silent period. So, I guess my movie was ahead of its time.

Eventually, *A Walk Beside Eden* got shown in front of an audience, about six years after I wrapped on it.

I didn't think I'd do another film so quickly, but around that time, there was a reality show I followed closely called *On the Lot*. The show, produced by Mark Burnett and Steven Spielberg, featured 50 contestants who had one week to make three-minute short films. The remaining 18 contestants teamed up and competed against each other, screening their resulting films each week. Viewers called in and voted for their favorite filmmakers. It was *Survivor* and *American Idol*, but with a filmmaking twist. The short films were a lot of fun, but the main reason I watched was to see who the weekly guest judge was. Aside from series regulars Garry Marshall and Carrie Fisher, there was always a guest director who showed up to judge that week's films. These ranged from Wes Craven, to Michael Bay, to Eli Roth. The grand prize was a million-dollar development deal with DreamWorks, with the winner getting to meet Steven Spielberg at the end of the show's finale. It was like watching someone else living my dream.

Don't remember the show? It only lasted for one season due to poor ratings and negative criticism, but had it continued past its initial run, they could have further developed it into something special. There's a good possibility that perhaps the general public doesn't care about how a film gets made. Also, some of the judges were particularly nasty, without giving any real constructive criticism. One of the harshest comments came from Princess Leia herself, who, after watching one of the contestants' horror films, said, "That was my least favorite thing next to adolescence and being left by a man for a man." Ouch.

But my favorite piece of criticism came from Michael Bay. Keep in mind, this was 2007, when he was still promoting his first *Transformers* movie. After watching one of the three-minute films, he commented that the filmmaker took a two-minute film and stretched it into three minutes. That's funny. I saw *Transformers*. Bay took a two-minute film and stretched it into three *hours*.

All that aside, the show inspired me to make a movie in less than twenty-four hours. I heard about the 48 Hour Film Project, and I even went to one of their introductory get-togethers, but never participated. Typically, with one of these competitions, you're required to meet rigid guidelines, and you don't get to pick your subject. This was my opportunity to do whatever I wanted, the only guideline being that I had to finish it in one day. That included writing, directing, shooting, and editing the whole film.

I remembered back to fourth grade, being a little nine-year-old boy, standing in front of my class and telling that engaging story about the time I walked home from school, had to chase after a quarter, and stomped on it until it became a pizza, rolling into the nearby sewer. To me, that made for exceptional visual storytelling. How would I pull that off?

With the miracle of editing.

After punching out a five-paged script, Matt agreed to come over and be the main actor. This was a big surprise, because Matt didn't like being on-camera. This was also the first film I was doing without Dan in some capacity.

As I waited for Matt, I borrowed a bunch of round objects from around the house and wrapped everything in tin foil. These would be my quarters. I had all the venues picked out. Now it was just a matter of getting it all filmed.

In *Loose Change*, Matt plays Luke Adayami, a lazy couch potato whose mom asks him to run to the store to get pizzas. As Luke starts walking down the sidewalk, he reaches into his pocket, only to find that his pockets have holes in them; and thus, he loses all the change he was supposed to use toward dinner.

He loses sight of all his change, except for a single quarter, which continues to roll down the sidewalk. As Luke chases after the sole coin, he notices with some confusion that the quarter appears to get bigger, like a snowball. As the film goes on, Luke continues chasing after the coin, almost getting hit by a car in the process, until finally the coin transforms into a pizza and slips through a manhole cover. Discouraged, Luke returns home, only to find that his mother got impatient and went to grab the pizzas herself. When she opens the pizzas, she is dismayed to find that they have been covered with random coins. It was a nice visual gag, and a creative way to end a fun concept, which I needed after finishing the incredibly somber tone of *Eden*.

The biggest challenge was getting the round objects, which were all covered in tin foil, to roll for longer than a second at a time. That's where the editing came in. In reality, we shot take after take of Matt attempting to roll quarters down the sidewalk. And small objects like coins don't film very well, especially against concrete, because they just blend in. It was accomplished by grabbing a series of wide and medium shots; the wide shots for Matt chasing the coin, and the medium shots containing just Matt, running toward something. Intercut together, it looks like he's constantly chasing this one object that keeps growing, and for the most part, it works.

It was written as a comedy, so the fact that you see the tin foil start to peel off some of the objects didn't really matter to me, so long as the intention was there. We even got the big coin (two garbage can lids taped together) to roll down a hill.

In the scene where the coin becomes a pizza and rolls into the sewer, I used a little smoke and mirrors. I used a jump cut to try and illustrate what happened. Then, I grabbed a shot of Matt looking down into the sewer cover. For this little feat, I cut rectangular slits in one of the pizza boxes and had Matt hold it up to his face. I've seen a lot worse.

By 11:00 that night, I had a finished cut of the film, which I edited on my laptop at the same dining room table where I filmed the climactic "pizza unveiling". You can see my laptop in the shot, proving once again that set dressing means nothing to me. For music, I "borrowed" tracks from James Venable's *Jay and Silent Bob Strike Back* score, which complements the film brilliantly.

Just the fact that we got *Loose Change* finished in one day was a huge accomplishment. It was also the strongest example of my skills as an editor. To this day, it's the one film I love showing people, because it's short, but it also has a fast pace, and it's funny. And it shows off a lot of technical skill. It's one of my better moments as a filmmaker.

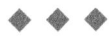

Since I graduated film school, my dream was to make feature films. I had ideas, and I even began working on scripts, but there was always something that prevented me from moving forward. Either I'd lose interest midway through a story, or I'd be faced with the daunting task of having to produce it. Usually, I'd get to a certain point where I realized no matter what grand ideas I had, I'd need a large amount of capital to pull off a film. I wasn't going to get it by working in retail.

By 2009, two years after I finished *A Walk Beside Eden* and *Loose Change*, I wasn't anywhere closer to pursuing my dream. I was still making YouTube videos, most of which only got a few views, and the few people who took the time to watch my videos weren't shy about letting me know how bad they sucked. I had a certificate in film as well as an Associates in Computer Science, and I wasn't finding work in either of those fields. My bills continued to mount, and as time went on, the possibility of becoming a filmmaker seemed to fade further into dreams, becoming a less likely scenario. I thought about going back to writing, which was what got me interested in filmmaking in the first place. But whenever I started a draft, I got frustrated because it felt like I was abandoning my dream. I firmly believed I was meant to be a filmmaker. I refused to let it go.

One day, Amanda came to visit me at Bullseye's. She was in tears. She never came to my work that upset. My heart sank, because deep down, I knew what she was going to tell me. It was the very thing people in my position dread hearing. I braced myself.

Amanda was pregnant.

CHAPTER 13:

Bullseye's? More Like Bull$@%t!

T wo weeks later, Amanda and I were at the Justice of the Peace, signing our marriage license. Her sisters threw us a reception at a VFW hall. Talk about a shotgun wedding. Our daughter, Alyssa, was born on March 16, 2010. In the months leading up to her birth, we went insane. I dreaded the future. Some of our family members were disappointed with us, while others were happy for us, but everyone wanted to chime in with their two cents about how we were going to have to change the course of our lives to accommodate a child.

Amanda's oldest sister said I needed to stop dreaming about filmmaking, go out and find a decent paying job. Even before Amanda came to me with the news that I swear made my heart stop in my chest, I wasn't pursuing film as much. I was desperately trying to get promoted at Bullseye's. By the time Alyssa was born, I had been an employee there for three years. I didn't know what else to do for money, so I decided that if I couldn't find a career that I was passionate about, I should just try to embrace the one I already had and make the best of it.

Eventually, my managers decided to take me under their wings and condition me for a leadership position. The pay was still lousy, but my hope, much had it been with Farmer Jack, was to get into a comfortable position and still be able to pursue my passions.

Once Ally was born, my only concern was keeping her clothed and fed. Filmmaking, at least as a career, was the farthest thing from my mind. I tried for a year after graduating college to find a decent IT job, but it seemed like I was running into the same thing: companies wanted kids with a lot of experience, and because my Associates allowed me to dabble in a lot of subjects but didn't really have a focus on anything, it seemed that my only course of action was to pursue further schooling. At $11 an hour, on top of trying to support a family, that wasn't going to happen.

Bullseye's started sending me out for interviews as a team lead. I always questioned my future, asking what the next steps were toward a promotion. The day I finally interviewed with the district manager, I was nervous and uptight. I made sure my red button-up shirt was ironed and tucked in tightly to my freshly washed Khakis. I was confident, and I liked the DM enough, but I had no idea how to read him.

One of the questions I asked him was what he was looking for in an executive, which was the position *ahead* of the one I was applying for. His response? "You'll need a Bachelors. You don't necessarily need a degree in business, but a Bachelor's shows us you have the ability to think."

❖ ❖ ❖

Leadership was tough. It was clear to me, even after I got the position, that I wouldn't be working at my current store. I was looking forward to working at the same location that championed me. I knew and respected most of the employees, and it would have been an easier transition.

As it so happened, I ended up transferring to a smaller store. There were less employees, which meant fewer resources to draw from. I would have to work twice as hard to get things done.

On my first day, the human resources manager took me out to lunch, and told me that a lot of the employees had "strong personalities."

A week later, I realized what she meant. And if I had been her, I would have chosen my words a little more carefully. Typically, celebrities are who I think of when I think "strong personalities." Movie stars, musicians, hell, even your local news anchor, have "strong personalities".

The employees at this store were just assholes.

I didn't get along with many of them. They were set in their ways, and they weren't ready to accept a new boss. Either they felt extremely comfortable telling me to where to stick it, or they were already at each other's throats. My boss pulled me aside and told me on day one who the troublemakers were.

It didn't help that while I knew most of Bullseye's core processes, I knew next to nothing about management. Even when I was a department head at Farmer Jack, I was a task-oriented supervisor, focusing more on getting my job completed than on supervising.

This became evident from the get-go. My supervisors, the executives, grew fond of telling me that I was "reactive instead of proactive," which basically meant I would only respond to a problem when there *was* a problem. And to a certain extent, that was true. I responded to feedback, even incredibly harsh feedback, and I tried to improve. But usually, I found myself either overcompensating or under-delivering, with no idea how to reach a comfy medium.

I was called into my supervisor's office so often (typically twice a week, for a "status update" – what I later referred to as an ass-chewing), that I rapidly started to lose confidence in myself. I became indecisive, which drove my employees crazy. Other times, I had a hard time delegating. I was still used to being a regular employee, so I tried to do all the necessary tasks myself. But then, a ton of other things got missed. We fell so far behind, often times I had to call on people from other departments to help get us caught up, which frustrated not only those employees, but the other team leads, who were unable to run their own departments.

It felt like a juggling act, and every day, the store would add more balls. The two-dollar-an-hour raise no longer seemed worth all the headache and aggravation, and I no longer had any ambition to grow with the company. My employees hated me, often going above my head to complain about me to the store manager, whether it was warranted or not. My supervisors were always second-guessing me, questioning my decisions, and there never seemed to be a good time to sit and read my emails. Oftentimes, when there was an important rollout, I completely dropped the ball.

On one occasion, my supervisor asked me if I had ever been diagnosed with a behavioral disorder. It was at that moment I realized: this was no longer about me not being equipped to do my job.

My bosses actually thought I was intentionally acting out, failing on purpose.

◆ ◆ ◆

Within a year, things at Bullseye's escalated, and I had no intentions of getting another promotion. At that point, I was just trying to keep my job.

That same year, I heard of a partnership between my alma mater, MPI, and Lawrence Technological University. My credits from MPI could be transferred over to Lawrence Tech and be used toward a Bachelor's in Media and Communications.

At twenty-nine-years-old, with a wife and a kid, the last thing I wanted to do was go back to college. The last two times I attended school, I got degrees only to chase my tail. And I certainly didn't want to accrue any more debt. In July that year, Amanda and I bought our first house, so I was already way over my head. I didn't think I could handle any more financial responsibility.

But I still knew this was an opportunity. And if I was going to go back to school, it should at least be for a subject I was interested in pursuing. A decade before, when I attended MPI, I was a young eighteen-year-old with a grand vision of making it as a filmmaker. I realized years later that that was a tall order.

I recalled what my parents told me when I decided to pursue film: try to at least pursue a more reasonable goal, such as broadcasting. All these years later, that didn't seem like a bad idea.

◆ ◆ ◆

I met with my student advisor, a pleasantly upbeat woman named Jody, who completely understood where I was coming from. Jody had worked in Hollywood for a number of years, and most recently worked as an art department coordinator on Wes Craven's *Scream 4*, which was partially filmed in Michigan. The first thing I noticed when I walked into her office was the fake DVD set of the *Stab* series, which was the film-within-a-film that permeated throughout the *Scream* films. She also had Sydney Prescott's novel, *Out of Darkness,* prominently displayed on her bookshelf. All of the pages were blank, as it was just a prop used in the film, but I was giddy, nonetheless.

Jody was impressed when she looked up my prior transcripts and realized I was mostly an A student. She was also curious how I was going to manage school, a family, and a full-time job.

I didn't know how, but I knew that I tended to do well in school, and I didn't plan on working in retail for the rest of my life. If I had to put myself through four years of Hell to get my degree, then that's what I was going to do.

I reapplied for financial aid, and was awarded enough grant money to get through my first semester. Each year, I filled out my financial aid packet, only to get awarded more grants. It seemed that the only condition for getting full coverage was to keep my grades up, which pushed me harder than ever to succeed.

It was both puzzling and rewarding, given how hard I was failing at my job. In a strange way, even my failures at work inspired me to do my best at school. Here I was, getting all A's, working on four-to-six hours of sleep sometimes, just to make sure my projects were done on time, or that I excelled at my midterms. It was a way of shoving all that bullshit back into my boss's face. How could I be failing so hard at one thing, yet excelling at another?

Because I didn't want to be at Bullseye's. Bullseye's was a way to make money. It allowed me to provide for my family. But I wasn't a good fit there. I excelled at school because the idea of getting a better-than-retail job propelled me to succeed, no matter how early I was in my college career.

◆ ◆ ◆

During my second year, I met Phil, a professional videographer who taught videography and editing. I took his Introduction to Video course, a requirement for my degree. As expected, the class focused more on electronic news gathering, which was more in line with the things I did in high school. I had to step out of my comfort zone, because most of my projects involved going to live events and grabbing interviews from complete strangers.

This never got any easier. Even when I scheduled the interviews well in advance, when I got to the location and set up my camera, I had a hard time relaxing. A lot of it had to do with my insecurities. I was unsure of myself. Even though I made short films and taped a dozen weddings, interviewing people made me uncomfortable. It felt like the person I interviewed was closely monitoring my every move, judging my professionalism and my knowledge of the camera – even though they more than likely didn't care, and just wanted to get it over with.

Despite my insecurities, I passed all the assignments with flying colors. Phil really liked a lot of my shots, because they weren't just floating heads filmed against a white background. And whereas some of the students struggled to find interesting venues, I went out of my way to find things that were at least interesting. I filmed one of my assignments at a carnival, and although it didn't come together as well as it should have (the carnival was held in October, when it was thirty degrees out, so there was barely anyone in attendance), it made for some interesting photography.

I also filmed at a local toy and comic book convention, which was right up my alley. The people running the con were very generous, more than happy to give an interview because hey, it was free press. There was even a surprise appearance from Darth Vader and a couple of Stormtroopers.

The following semester, I took Phil's editing class. Lawrence Tech provided students with laptops for whatever majors required them. The media comm students all had access to Macs, the industry standard for creative applications. That meant I had access to one of the most popular pieces of editing software, Final Cut Pro.

Right from the get-go, I was teaching myself the software, editing not only my class assignments, but my personal movie reviews. At the start of every class, I had a new video ready to go, showing it to Phil so I could get his feedback. He was impressed at how quickly I was learning the software.

Before Final Cut, I used Sony Vegas. It was a powerful piece of software, available exclusively for PCs, which might have been the reason why big production houses never really adopted it. It's ironic how today, PCs are just as common as Macs due to the flexibility of the hardware and the lower price tags. But even back in 2013, most people in the video and media industry swore by Macs, and Final Cut was a big player in that arena.

I spent so much time editing with Vegas, that by the time I transitioned over to Final Cut, it was almost second nature.

Essentially, once you learn how to use one NLE (non-linear editor), learning the next one is much easier. In fact, I had more trouble adapting to the Mac operating system than I did with Final Cut. I grew up in a PC household. I was used to Windows. Learning how to operate a Mac took some patience. And I'm not trying to be a PC snob. Mac is a fine operating system. It's just, when you spend all your life driving an automatic, and then someone shows you how to drive a stick for the first time, it takes some getting used to.

My final assignment in editing class was to put together a five-minute piece Phil shot. He and his fishing buddy went up to the Muskegon River to do some fly fishing. Phil taped the entire trip, with his buddy Jim explaining the process. I'm not sure if Phil had a narrative in mind, but my job was to scan through the footage and find one.

I made more than a dozen passes on the video, anxiously showing each cut to Phil. Again, he was impressed with how efficiently I was putting it together, not to mention all the time and care I was putting into the project.

One night, Phil needed a ride to his work, a couple miles away from campus. On the way there, Phil asked if I would be interested in interning with his company. I'm pretty sure he knew my answer before he even propositioned me.

◆ ◆ ◆

Even though it was an unpaid internship, working for Phil's company was a dream come true. Twice a week, I left Bullseye's early so I could drive across town and edit a piece Phil was working on for a client. Before I left, I made a point to change in the men's room, just so my fellow employees could see me in nice casual clothes. I would grin and wave at them, then cheerfully run out of the building, eccentric to go from my crappy paying job to my awesome non-paying gig.

I also got to help out on shoots, mostly as a production assistant. Again, I was mostly responsible for hefting around equipment and micing talent. Occasionally, though, Phil wanted me to set up lights and position the camera. He gave me a specific setup, and then he would leave the room to prep the talent.

Typically, when I shot my own things, I was used to hand-held shots, and because I didn't have access to my own lighting packages, I used natural lighting. I hadn't worked much in a professional capacity, and lighting was always a struggle for me. I either tended to under- or overexpose, again failing to meet that middle ground.

I always feel like lighting a shot is this extreme thing, used to give this grand look that only masters can achieve. What I didn't realize was, not all lighting has to be dramatic. Sometimes it's subtle.

Either way, despite taking Phil's videography class, I still wasn't comfortable with the three-light setup. I just hadn't done it enough to feel confident.

But here's the thing about Phil: if he believed in your skills, he was more than happy to work with you. I worked with a lot of people who were condescending. They might yell and berate me, or at the very least, they would question a decision I made. Phil never did that. If I forgot how to do something, he would take the time out to retrain me. He *instructed* me, much as he did in his capacity as a professor. He was always patient, because he knew I had it in me. He was familiar with my work. Sometimes, I felt like he was testing me, putting me in a position where I had to apply what he taught in class. After all, technically, this was for college credit. This wasn't a job offering, it was essentially another class, but one where I was getting hands-on training.

There were even times where Phil took suggestions from me. We were shooting a piece for a retirement home, and we were scouting a location for a specific shot. This was a nice facility, and outside, there was a decorative rock water fountain. I suggested we set our next interview against the fountain. Phil framed the shot with his hands, and within minutes, we had the next shot setup and ready to go.

By the end of the semester, there weren't any full-time positions available. However, for the next few years, Phil would occasionally contact me for freelance work, in which I *was* paid. It wasn't making movies, but those were some of the best jobs I ever had.

CHAPTER 14:

A Trial of Errors

In February of 2013, Amanda was pregnant with our second child. I figured I was about two months away from getting fired at Bullseye's, I was still working for slave wages, and I was three years away from finishing school.

In between working and taking classes, I attempted to go back to writing, but there were too many distractions. Making movies seemed futile because I didn't have the energy to look for actors, scout locations, let alone set aside time to go into production. Everything I did from that point on was for my family.

Even though I was focusing more on the corporate end of things, whenever I had the chance to work on something creative, I applied myself. I started to build my reputation as an editor, so on most assignments, I was automatically designated as the group editor.

One semester, the entire class had to turn in a single piece as our final assignment. The class was taught by a producer at one of the big local television studios. As a class, we decided to produce a fifteen-minute "pilot" episode called *College Code*, where we got several college students to engage in humorous conversations regarding their perceptions of college life. Segments of their conversations would be intertwined with little sketches to illustrate the topics.

All of the interviews were shot in the college's studio against a green screen. One of the students was responsible for creating animations that I later dropped into the backgrounds in post. It was insane, because the entire class project depended on my editing skills, and with everything else that was going on in my personal life, it was like running a marathon.

There really is no greater feeling than working hard on something and presenting it to an audience. My classmates were incredibly supportive throughout the whole process, and seeing it come together as a group was a great experience.

I also got to work on a short film, this time solely as a writer. Our groups had to pick a piece of dialogue out of a hat, and we had to incorporate it into our finished piece, as well as make the single line of dialogue the theme. We ended up making a mockumentary about a twenty-seven-year-old man who aspired to join the Girl Scouts.

This was where some of my experience as a filmmaker was invaluable. The students always relied on tripods, for *every-thing*. In my opinion, tripods are really only necessary for interviews. That doesn't mean everything needs to be handheld, but when you're doing a documentary, you really need to free up your hands and *move* the camera. Tripods are great for static shots. But if you create a shot where the camera needs to dolly in for a tighter angle, or you need to truck in a certain direction, a tripod gets in the way.

We were shooting our film on a professional-grade video camera, the kind you can comfortably rest on your shoulders. No one could trust that I could pull off a steady handheld shot, and they all insisted that I put the camera on sticks and simply move the camera when the scene required movement. After the shots failed several times, I pleaded with my fellow classmates to let me hold the camera and pull off the moves we needed, and guess what? Our little movie started coming together.

The film also taught me how to be more collaborative. In the film, we interviewed the parents of our protagonist. Humorously, the mother character stood by her son and supported his every decision. The father character was fiercely conservative, and was almost ashamed of his son, wishing he had played football as opposed to pursuing a career with the Girl Scouts.

We intentionally kept our protagonist's sexual orientation ambiguous, but the father character came off dangerously close to being bigoted, and that was understandably a problem. We didn't want to offend anyone.

One of my classmates had a more delicate sensibility, and we couldn't agree on the original ending. She wanted the father character to finally come to terms with his son's choice, and at the end of the story, she felt he should join his son at his awards ceremony, after getting accepted into the organization. I tried explaining that if we made that choice, there wouldn't be an obstacle for our protagonist to overcome.

If you have a soft heart and a level head, and you like to create things, it's difficult to think up nasty things to put your characters through. But that's how drama works. Imagine if in *Star Wars*, instead of Darth Vader destroying the planet Alderaan, he actually listened to Princess Leia's pleas and decided he was going to sketch out a living designing model airplanes instead? It might make for a funny SNL skit, but it's not going to sell tickets.

As the writer, I felt very close to the story of this film, and I wanted it to work. But I wanted my classmates to feel that they had a say in it, too. So, I asked her to come up with something better, something that still realized the father as an antagonist, but that wasn't altogether despicable: a middle ground.

And she did.

Again, our film was shown in front of an audience, and it was a delightful experience.

Not everything I did was met with acclaim, though.

Thankfully, because it was college, I had room to experiment. One of the hardest projects I worked on was a commercial that promoted – are you ready for this?

The resurgence in Detroit.

Detroit is known as a dangerous city. Growing up, my parents dreaded going anywhere near it, and they always warned me about going there. I have an aunt who, to this day, lives downtown. Growing up, if my mom wanted to spend the day with her, she would have to take a bus, and my mom would go pick her up from the bus station.

It didn't help that the former mayor of Detroit, Kwame Kilpatrick, had been brought up on multiple criminal charges and was the subject of several sex and murder scandals.

I didn't follow the news in detail, but doing a commercial promoting Detroit didn't really seem like a viable project. Especially since actually going down to *film* it would be a requirement.

I came up with a premise, having no idea how to go about producing it. The concept was that an outgoing well-to-do family was visiting Detroit as tourists, and throughout the spot, after visiting some of the more recognizable landmarks, Detroit would transform them into a "hipper" family.

I had storyboards and an entire marketing campaign built around the concept. But I still had no idea how I was going to go about filming it.

That was the year it rained almost every day. Every time I went downtown to pick out shots, it rained. As the deadline got closer, I started to panic, so I went down with my camera and interviewed random people who lived in the city. And one of those people happened to be homeless.

I put together a quick spot with some voiceovers, more

out of desperation than anything else, and showed it to my professor. And as expected, he was furious.

It would have been better just to not turn anything in. I gave him a concept that he was sold on, and what I turned in was the complete opposite of what he asked for. This wasn't a resurgence, it was confirming what people already thought of Detroit: a homeless man giving his two cents about the community, followed by, and I'm not making this up: a shot of Canada. Yes, I was trying to end with a shot of the Detroit River, but I shot *across* the river. And if you live in Detroit, you know that if you look across the Detroit River, you'll see Canada.

This wasn't my final project. It was something I lumped together *in case* I wouldn't be able to put my final piece together. I was having a hard time finding a clear shooting day, and I couldn't find actors.

Finally, I asked Amanda, my dad, and Matt to help me out. They dressed up in tropical clothes, then grabbed their winter jackets and their umbrellas, which completely covered up their colorful wardrobes, and together we drove out to Detroit in one of the rainiest days of the year.

It also didn't help that I practically had to beg Matt to help out. He had no interest in driving out. I explained to him that if there was ever a time I needed a favor from him, this was it. He simply wouldn't help.

"I'm going to remember this," I said.

And he finally came out.

My dad couldn't walk very far at that point, so the only way he'd be able to be in the spot was by driving around in his motorized scooter. And it wasn't hard to tell, just by looking at him, that he was handicapped. It was a questionable casting choice that detracted from the upbeat family aspect I originally intended.

We screened this first attempt in class, and there was

no shortage of criticism. The students knew what I was trying to pull off, but it didn't come through because the wardrobe wasn't there – remember, everyone was wearing their winter coats – and there was nothing that popped about it. It still wasn't shouting "resurgence." In the spot, everyone was visiting the famous Joe Louis Fist, Cobo Arena, and Greektown, but that's all that was happening. There wasn't a real story.

The professor started to lose hope in my project, and that was a shame, because very rarely had I turned in a bad project. I was working my ass off to get this thing made, and I kept disappointing. This is why my respect for movie critics has diminished over the years.

I was determined to turn in a good product, even if my professor seemed to give up on me. So, I reshot the whole damn thing.

I brought in the cast of *A Walk Beside Eden*. And by cast, I mean myself and Amanda. I asked my friend Scott, a Lawrence Tech alum and part-time advisor, to do all the shooting, and I let him choose most of the shots. We finally got a day where it wasn't raining, although it was still windy as all get out, so we were able to show off our goofy tourist clothes.

In the span of one evening, I had all the footage I needed to put together a commercial. It was one of the most compromised pieces I ever worked on, but I finally had something I was confident enough in to hand in as a final piece.

I got a fellow classmate to record a voiceover that flowed throughout the length of the piece, accompanied by a generic hip-hop score, and ending on a slick animated logo of the 'D' from Detroit. The professor was impressed by the amount of effort that went into it, and didn't expect me to go back out and reshoot the entire piece. Keep in mind, I was working two jobs, I had a kid on the way, and I had other classes to think about. This was a huge undertaking, and the fact that I walked away with an 'A' was baffling, yet satisfying as hell.

One of the last classes I took was a technical writing class, taught by Phil's wife, Beth. I worked with Beth on a few freelance gigs, but she basically knew me as a technical guy. She wasn't familiar with my background as a writer.

Over time, Beth confided in me that if she had an open position available, she would be confident in hiring me as a professional writer. She was surprised at what I turned in.

It was that praise that brought me back full circle to my first passion.

CHAPTER 15:

*A Case of "What the $@!
% Do I Do Now?!"*

In the span of two months, two important changes took place. On November 4th, 2013, Amanda gave birth to our son, David. And at the beginning of January, Bullseye's fired me.

I walked into the building that day, depressed as I'd ever been. Regardless, I had my day's work all cut out, and despite wanting to put a gun to my head, I walked in with a smile in my heart and a confident stride.

Then my manager asked me to meet in her office.

Typically, when I received a "status update," I received a large packet that listed all of the things I did wrong. This time, my manager didn't hand me the packet, but the words "Notice of termination" were typed prominently, in bold, on the front page.

I looked at my manager. "Is this my last day?" I asked.

She nodded, as she started reading me my termination notice. I knew this was coming for a long time, and truth be told, I was kind of shocked they kept me around as long as they did.

As I drove home that morning, the first thing I felt was stress. What was I going to tell Amanda? We had a two-month-old infant at home, and I could barely make ends meet.

Then, slowly, a wave of relief swept over me. I *hated* working for Bullseye's. They were an awful company to work for. I didn't get along with any of my co-workers, and most of my fellow leaders wanted me gone.

Because it was just a retail job, I shouldn't have cared. It was just a job. But it was the first time I had ever been fired. I felt like I let my family down. I couldn't understand why I crashed and burned as hard as I did. Every day with that company was a complete struggle.

I have mixed feelings about my experience there. On the one hand, I felt that I was mostly bullied. My peers didn't want to help me succeed, they just wanted to beat me up and kick me to the ground whenever I failed. It was a very American sentiment. Everything was cutthroat, with all the team leads trying to stab each other in the back, all for a little advancement opportunity.

On the other hand, I let my team down. I wasn't a good manager. I had a difficult time making firm decisions, and at one point, I even tried to win them over with donuts as opposed to my own managerial charm. Essentially, I was used to working as an employee, doing all the hands-on stuff. And because of my past retail experience, I was typically good with people, which was what prompted a few of the executives to condition me for leadership in the first place.

But I was, and still am, an introvert. Telling people what to do doesn't come natural to me. That doesn't mean I'm incapable of supervising. Believe me, if the time ever comes when I'm able to walk onto a film set and act as a director, I'll rise to the occasion.

The point I'm trying to make is, when you're working for a place that you have absolutely no passion for, it's difficult –

maybe even impossible – to do your best. Bullseye's brought out the worst in me.

It was then that I made it my goal to never work in the retail industry again. Getting fired from Bullseye's was a blessing in disguise. Now I could truly pursue a career in something I was good at.

Two months later, I found myself working at Groker – a grocery retailer.

◆ ◆ ◆

I was still pursuing my Bachelors at Lawrence Tech, but as the program was more geared toward communications and broadcasting, there weren't a lot of opportunities to pursue film.

Then one of my colleagues, a filmmaker herself, developed the Broke Student Film Festival as her senior project. It was a one-night event where students who had dabbled in filmmaking could showcase their work. I submitted two pieces: *Attack of the B Movies* and *Loose Change.*

I was taking Phil's Intro to Video course, and he took the entire class down to the auditorium to see the films. When we got back later that night, one of the students criticized *Loose Change* for its amateur cinematography, not knowing it was my film. I sat and listened to his critique, with a little half-smile on my face. The criticism hurt, sure, but I enjoyed being a fly on the wall for that.

Over the next few years, the event actually grew into a fully-fledged film festival. Students from all over the world were submitting their films for consideration. It stretched from this small two-hour viewing party to a three-day event, and the competition was fierce. This was no longer a place for amateurs. There were serious filmmakers who were showcasing their work, and overnight, my films seemed to get buried in the shuffle.

I consider myself a decent storyteller. I can shoot something, put it together, and be able to convey a story. But I'm not necessarily a techie, nor am I graphically talented. Most of these filmmakers knew their way around After Effects, and a lot of the films being shown showcased their technical capabilities.

During the second year of the festival, I submitted *A Walk Beside Eden*. It was the first time the film was being shown to the public. If I had any film that I was actually proud to show off, that would be it.

In order for the film to get accepted, I had to cut it down to ten minutes. That meant that two-thirds of the film had to go. *A Walk Beside Eden*, in its entirety, is about a guy who has to come to terms with death. That was the point of having the father character die early on, so the audience would wonder about the outcome of Eden.

Obviously, at ten minutes, I had to focus on the relationship between the two characters. Also, for legal reasons, I had to ditch my temp music track. *Eden,* being a silent film, relies on music to tell the story. It was the emotional center of the film, and if the music doesn't work, the story isn't as powerful.

Unfortunately, I couldn't afford to hire a composer, so I had to resort to finding royalty-free music, which is almost never great.

That year, on top of submitting my film, I also volunteered to work at the festival. This included finding sponsors, as well as collecting ballots at the end of the screenings from the audience, who would vote on things such as "Best Film".

Somehow, I forgot that my film was showing that night, and I got to see the judges tally up all the votes. Out of the twenty films that screened, *A Walk Beside Eden* was the only film that didn't get a single vote.

There were a couple of films that got one or two votes, but *Eden* got none. It was a total eye opener.

There may have been several reasons why the film didn't work for people. One of the comments actually stated that the music was too loud. I found that kind of strange, but I also made the film before I started attending Lawrence Tech, which was where I learned how to sweeten my audio to an appropriate level. I also shot the film on a consumer-level mini-DV camcorder, whereas most of the other filmmakers shot on DSLRs, which were quickly growing in popularity because of their interchangeable lenses and sharp picture quality.

I tried to not let it discourage me, but as time went on, I started to doubt myself. I dreamed for years of being a filmmaker. Here I was, in my thirties. I had a house, two kids, a wife, and I was *still* clinging to that dream. Could it be – was I just not any good?

Around this time, I was really struggling with where to direct my passions. Should I continue to pursue filmmaking, or go back to writing? After all, that's where it all started. It seemed that either way, making a career out of either one was going to be a difficult road.

This was my dilemma: I almost never read books, unless they were assigned in class, or they were a graphic novel. The only time I really ever picked up a book was if the subject matter was incredibly engaging to me, such as an autobiography on George Lucas or Andy Kaufman. You would think as much as I loved writing science fiction, I'd be reading every *Star Wars* novel I could get my hands on. But to this day, I have an entire shelf full of unread *Star Wars* novels from the 90's.

On the other side of that, I *love* to watch movies. But making movies is the hardest artform imaginable, because you need an army of people, and more importantly, you need money. There are certainly filmmakers who will tell you that you don't need either, and yes, I suppose you can grab a group of friends who are willing to work for free, find a remote cabin in the woods, and suffer for your art – it has happened. But let's be honest. In today's economy, no one wants to work for free. And if you're really serious about filmmaking, it's work.

It's moving lights, furniture, and props. It's a lot of set dressing, painting, and decorating. And once you shoot your scenes, you tear it all down, you move to the next location, and you do it all over again.

The most professional film I ever made, *Attack of the B Movies*, was the least fun I had making a movie. I guess it really depends on the concept, and that film used a lot of makeup and some special effects. And there were other contributing factors.

But I was at a point in my life where I couldn't expect to have fun *and* make a living. If I was going to pursue my passions, it would have to be on my own time. Trying to make a career out of an artform just hadn't been working for me. I couldn't support my family by making movies.

So, I decided, if I had extra time, I would try really hard to make movies. Or I would write something. But either way, I needed something to pay the bills. I didn't want to keep going back to college, because Lawrence Tech was expensive enough as it was.

What I needed was a decent paying full-time job, something that I didn't hate, that I could just do, come home from, and pursue my passions afterwards. That was now my focus.

CHAPTER 16:

One Final Pipe Dream

I was checking my email when I received a message from the Post Office. It was a hiring letter asking me to come in and take some kind of a test – the first step to being hired in. I didn't even remember applying.

After passing the entrance exam, it was off to training at the postal academy. I was taught how to sort mail, I learned a lot of the postal lingo, and I even went through driver's training, learning how to handle the mail truck.

I know what you're thinking. What does this have anything to do with filmmaking?

Not a damn thing. Neither did Groker, and neither did Bullseye's. But I had a family to support. If you've been paying attention this far, you might recall that I tried for the past two decades to find a way of make a living out of my passions, and I hadn't succeeded. I was in my early thirties, and even facing the tail-end of college, I really didn't expect to get a decent video production job.

The Post Office was the first job I had where I could say the pay was halfway decent. I wouldn't have to deal with a slew of whiny customers when I was out delivering. While delivering packages didn't seem ideal in the wintertime, it seemed like a pretty kick-ass gig in the summertime.

There was one caveat, however. Like most rookie postal carriers, I would be hired in part-time, as a sub. Being a sub at the Post Office is very much like being a substitute teacher, in that you're a fill-in. When one of the regulars calls in sick, you get called in to fill the route. Which meant that at the very beginning, you're only guaranteed to work two days out of the month.

Fortunately, I still had my job at Groker. So, I made an arrangement: I would keep my days open in case the Post Office needed me, and work at Groker in the evenings.

This was both a blessing and a curse. Obviously, during the weeks that the Post Office was fully staffed, having that second job was a godsend. Then again, during the summer when everyone took their vacation, working both jobs was a pain in the ass.

Starting a new job is never easy. Aside from a learning curve, there's a pretty good chance you're going to butt heads with people who frankly, don't want you there. I'll be honest – as of this writing, I sincerely enjoy working as a rural mail carrier. But looking back, there were times where I didn't think it was a good fit.

Let's start with the location. I live about five minutes from St. Claire Shores, which is where I thought I was going to be working. I didn't know that there was a St. Clair *township* that was forty minutes away. And *that's* where I ended up working.

The morning commute aside, I didn't know the area. When I first started delivering out that way, I was constantly getting lost and always GPSing where to go, which slowed me down. Also, something a lot of people don't understand: those mail trucks are old as shit. The Post Office would just as soon keep fixing them than replace them. Some of those trucks are over twenty years old, and they're always breaking down. On the first week of the job, every time I was in the middle of my route, my truck stalled. I thought maybe I was doing something wrong. I typically pay attention in class, but I didn't remember them saying anything about a kill switch. And whenever the truck broke down, I'd have to call my supervisor, who then had to send other carriers out to give me a hand while I waited for a tow truck to come and swap out my vehicle.

I also hated learning the routes. Unfortunately, in order to get hours, it's a necessity. It was hard enough learning my primary route, let alone everyone else's.

Toward the beginning, during the holiday season, I was out past five o'clock – and I had a class that night! On the night of my final exam, I was out and about, in the dark, delivering parcels in St. Clair, when I had to be in Southfield within the hour – a fifty-mile hike.

I frantically tried calling my professor on the way in, who was undoubtedly in the middle of presentations. It didn't help that I had to stop home to grab a nice button-up shirt. And I still showed up to class with torn blue jeans, which didn't make my group look good.

On top of learning the ins-and-outs of the Post Office and finishing up college, I was also working at Groker in the evenings. I worked in the deli, which I despised because I was nervous about working around prepared foods. It wasn't that I was incompetent about it, but I know how people can get when you're around their food. I had to change my gloves fifty times a night, and god forbid I should have to sneeze. Even though I used my sleeve, most customers who saw me didn't want me anywhere near their food.

It didn't help that my manager, a stringent, extremely OCD little woman – we'll call her 'R' – hated my guts. She rode me every chance she got. R was never happy with how I closed the department, even though the executives who walked the store every night admitted I was the best closer they had. There were two women in their late 50's who had worked there forever, and were slow as molasses. But because they had seniority, R left them to their own devices to fuck stuff up.

R was constantly hiring new people, because no one would stay past their initial 90-day training period. Most of the people she hired were either alcoholics lifted off the street, or kids still in high school who obviously didn't give a shit. And no matter how poor their work ethics were, R hated me most of all.

Because I never worked at the Post Office on Sundays (something that has changed in recent years because of Amazon), I was able to work the morning shift at Groker – after closing the previous Saturday. And every Sunday morning, R greeted me with a laundry list of complaints. The temps weren't taken correctly, the trash wasn't all taken out, the floors looked horrible, and she always managed to find a bit of grease or grime that I overlooked because I was too damn busy cleaning up everyone else's mess. She berated me in front of the customers, no matter how busy we were, and she was so over-dramatic! On many occasions, she actually slammed her fist down on the metal prep tables to prove her point.

One night, the store manager called me in to close because the deli was shorthanded. R had no idea I was coming in. I closed the entire department by myself, and it was spotless by the time I left.

The next night, I came in to close once again. I cleaned everything exactly as I had the night before. R always left a checklist so everyone could sign off on what they did that night. The previous night, because I was under pressure to close on my own, I forgot to sign off on it. However, she left a note saying how impressed she was with the department.

The third night, I came in and got into my usual routine. I noticed that she left a nasty note about how the department was closed the previous night. I should probably point out that I *had* signed off on the sheet this time, so she knew it had been me. She even went out of her way to take a photograph of one of the pieces I was responsible for cleaning.

I got called into the manager's office for a write-up.

I recalled all the times I had been called into the manager's office at Bullseye's, and how on many occasions I just sat in my chair feeling sorry for myself as my supervisor read off the list of things I fucked up on.

At Bullseye's, I was in a management position, and I'll admit, I was afraid of speaking out because I had a family and I really needed the job.

But I had worked at a grocery store when I was fresh out of high school. I hated – fucking *loathed* – that I was stuck working at one again, well into my thirties. At this point in my life, I simply didn't give a shit.

And thankfully, R left a paper trail behind.

I walked into the manager's office holding two pieces of paper – one with R's complementary note on the checklist I forgot to sign off on, and the other with her nasty comment, scribbled next to my signature. "This is bullshit," I told the store manager. "I cleaned the department the exact same way on both of these nights. The only reason she came down on me is because she hates me."

The manager took both sheets of paper and examined them. "I thought the department looked pretty good when I came in this morning," he said. "I just assumed someone else closed."

I shook my head. "She's been riding me ever since I started. You've seen me work. Does it look like I slack off? I come in and I know exactly what to do. *And,* I also train all the new hires because she doesn't schedule any time to train them herself. I don't know what her problem is, but there's proof that she's tagging me like a shark."

The store manager darted his eyes back and forth between the two checklists. He looked down at the write-up – *my* write-up – and right there in front of me, crumpled it up and tossed it in the wastepaper basket. "I'll have a talk with her," he said. "She can't just target you because she feels like it."

At the same time, R had an assistant, a backup supervisor who was on my side. She was a young Albanian woman named Jenna, and we always got along. Because Jenna was fairly new to the position, I caught her simply agreeing with everything R said. But eventually Jenna got the impression that I was locked in her sights, and she went to bat for me.

"I've seen how Lenny works, and trust me, he's not lazy," I heard Jenna say. "He works harder than everyone back here combined, and you need to stop trying to write him up because I need his help."

I never figured out what R's beef with me was. One time, she actually told me that she was holding me to a higher standard than everyone else, which made absolutely no sense. I was just a guy trying to scrape out a living so I could support my family, something I had been struggling with for years. I wasn't trying to win a gold medal or become super rich. I just wanted to make sure that my kids ate three meals a day and could go to bed with a roof over their heads.

Eventually, R transferred to another location, and the word on the playground was that Jenna was in the running to be the next deli manager. The store manager had several candidates in mind. By that point, I was getting ready to leave the company. R was absolutely miserable to work for. I walked into the store manager's office and told him point blank: if he hired Jenna, I would stay. I'm not sure if that had any influence on his decision, but guess who ended up being the next deli manager?

Life under Jenna's supervision became much more bearable. We got along perfectly. There were no more write-ups about the department not being clean, and when she hired in new people, she actually took my advice under consideration when it came to their performance.

Despite the change in management, I knew that I couldn't go on working there much longer. I was barely making ends meet, but between that, college, and the Post Office, I needed a break. I needed to make a change.

And you thought working two jobs and going to college wasn't enough? As I approached my final year of college, Jody sat me down and explained that she wanted to really grow my professional portfolio. She got me in touch with Sharon, the Director of Marketing for the college. Sharon quickly took me under her wing, developing a series of video projects I could helm that would ultimately promote the school and enhance my body of work.

Admittedly, even after three years of college and years of film work, I didn't have much in the way of a professional reel. Most of the things I had looked fairly amateurish. When it came to my films, it was all relative. I loved most everything I produced. But Jody and Sharon both felt that a short horror spoof wasn't going to go very far in finding me a job.

Before long, I found myself working for the marketing department as a video producer. That's right, folks – three jobs. The biggest ongoing project I worked on was a series of man-on-the-street segments called *LT Asks U*, where I approached total strangers – mostly incoming freshmen – and asked them random questions about life on campus. It was completely outside of my comfort zone, because I have always had a rough time talking to strangers. Keep in mind, this wasn't made any easier by the fact that I was carrying around a bunch of video equipment, which didn't make the talent any more comfortable. About one out of three students I approached were game to be interviewed. Once they agreed, I don't think they really understood the extent of the work until they actually saw me setting up the camera, hooking up the lav mic to their shirt collar, and testing out the gear before finally getting to the actual question of the day.

Over the years, I've learned one very crucial thing about myself: I vastly prefer editing to running camera. Although most of these segments came out fine, there was always an issue I had to overcome. Most of the time, I couldn't get the sound right. You would think all I had to do was make sure the microphone was pointed at the subject, but even between trying out different mics, there was always an issue, and I never perfected it.

You never want to use the built-in mic on the camera, because it sounds tinny, and you're always competing with whatever sound is in the background. I experimented with a miniature boom mic, a microphone built on a telescoping rig that can be suspended, off-camera, just inches from the talent's mouth. Usually this sounds pretty good, but when you're the only person shooting, it's just one extra element you have to be in charge of. Sometimes I would accidentally drop the mic in frame, and more often than not the connection was bad, so I wouldn't get anything.

I also experimented with a wireless lavalier, a button-sized mic that you can hook onto a piece of clothing and is virtually invisible. These are usually hit-or-miss for me, because there's so much involved with hooking it up. First, because it's a wireless system, you have to deal with both a receiver and a transmitter. The receiver gets hooked into the camera's audio jack, and you have to make sure the antenna is pointed in the right direction, usually at a 45-degree angle and directly at the talent. The transmitter gets hooked onto the talent, which can usually be clipped onto their waistline or belt. This is also where the mic itself is connected to. The trick is to try and hide the wire so that the audience sees as little of the mic as possible. If the talent is wearing a nice button-up shirt, this is easy: you can slip the mic through one of the button openings and clip it to their lapel or collar. If the talent is a college student wearing a tank top, this is much more challenging.

The most luck I had with recording sound was with a

$200 microphone I purchased myself. It ran on a 9-volt battery and provided pretty decent sound, provided the talent wasn't standing too far from the camera. Even with that setup, Sharon wasn't always enthusiastic with the result.

As far as being my boss, I found Sharon to be quite intimidating, but not in the way that my previous managers were. Sharon held me up to a high standard because she expected me to do no less than professional work. If what I turned in seemed like amateur-hour, she wasn't shy about expressing that. But I never felt like she was taking advantage of me or didn't want me around. Sharon was, first and foremost, a mentor.

Out of my four years at Lawrence Tech, I learned the most by working under her. She was extremely finicky about my choice of shots; not so much what I tried to achieve, but of what kinds of things I had in front of the lens. On several occasions, she would spot a trashcan or an undesirable, less-than-attractive artifact in frame that she trained me to look out for. It seems trivial, but do you remember a certain *Game of Thrones* episode where a Starbucks cup had actually been left in the background? And that was fucking *Game of Thrones*.

Sharon also taught me to get the most out of my backgrounds. To this day, whenever I see a video or even a still shot where someone is simply standing in front of a solid wall, I cringe. I used a lot of hallways in the beginning, because long corridors give you that nice depth of field. But after the twentieth hallway shot, Sharon taught me that there were other places on campus where I could take advantage of my surroundings. She showed me to utilize my space and really consider what I was shooting. As Jody would later put it, every frame should look like something you'd want to hang on your wall.

I'm not sure I completely agree with that philosophy – sometimes a cigar is just a cigar. But it definitely brought my camera skills to a heightened level, and from then on, whenever I attempted to put something on film, I took a look around before I set up the camera.

◆ ◆ ◆

As graduation was quickly approaching, the thought of not having to study, not having to dedicate every waking moment to a class project, not having to dart around between three jobs and classes, was a huge relief. Of course, something else happened that I inevitably would have to deal with.

I was on my way to my car, leaving for my morning class, when Amanda ran down the driveway screaming my name. The sound of her voice was blood-curdling. I thought someone was stabbing her to death.

As I got out of the car, I realized with terror that she was holding David – our two-year-old son – limply in her arms. He was barely breathing.

Amanda was too panicked to know what to do, so I ran into the house and called 9-1-1. I sat by David's side and tried talking to him. He was alive, and he was breathing slowly, but he looked confused. His face was turning blue. His head was covered with sweat, and he was burning up. Amanda found him on the floor of his bedroom, face down and not moving. She feared the worst.

Before the ambulance got to our house, David started shaking and convulsing. I was freaking out. Amanda was, too. But Amanda, from her own childhood experience, knew what it was. David was having a seizure.

Once the ambulance got there, David was breathing again, but he still looked confused. His eyes darted around as if he had no idea who we were. One of the paramedics got him a breathing apparatus, and before long the three of us were in the back of the ambulance. The paramedic tending to David explained to us that he was fine for the time being, but he had another seizure as they loaded him onto the gurney, so he was currently unstable.

Once at the hospital, we sat around waiting for a neurologist. In that time, David had another seizure. Amanda and I were completely panicked. Even Amanda had never experienced so many in such a short amount of time.

After hours of doctors hooking up leads to our son's head (Amanda and I both restraining his arms and legs to keep him from pulling them off), and after having an overnight EEG, the neurologist diagnosed him with genetic epilepsy.

Over the next few months, David's seizure medication increased, until they finally found the right dose to give him where his seizures would stabilize. He was having them about once a month by this point, but each one was incredibly scary. The neurologists warned us about some of the symptoms, as they didn't always have to appear as shaking convulsions – although most, if not all, of his seizures appeared that way. They warned us about any dazing off into space, or not being receptive to his surroundings, or if he simply broke off into a laughing fit. To my knowledge, none of these actually occurred. To a couple of new parents, this was an especially trying time.

The day of graduation came and went. It was bittersweet, because even though I was wearing the traditional cap and gown, and I finally had my much-sought-after Bachelor's degree, I had nothing lined up. If anything, I was exactly where I had been four years before, looking for a paying gig – except this time, I was ten-thousand dollars in debt.

Only ten-thousand dollars, you ask?

I graduated summa cum laude, with the highest grade-point average in my class. I think because of that, I was able to finance most of my schooling with academic scholarships. Sometimes being a poor parent has its advantages.

That's why, as much as I struggled at Bullseye's and at

Groker, I tried really hard not to take any of it personally. How could someone work three jobs, go to school three days a week, support a family, *and* come out with a 3.7 grade point average, be *that* much of a fuck up? It didn't make a lot of sense to me.

And at that point, it didn't matter. Even after the challenge of school ended, I still had to support my family. I still needed to work two jobs to make ends meet, and neither one had anything to do with what I went to school for. I was going to be working freelance for a really long time. Somehow, the idea of school ending made me more depressed than I had been in a while. The future didn't look all that bright. Once again, I felt like a failure.

That was the summer where I worked one last film job.

As usual, it was an unpaid internship, working as a production assistant on some shitty production. The only reason I considered taking the job was because they were shooting on a RED Epic camera, which is the system of digital cinematography used by major Hollywood studios.

As usual, I was talked down to by the production managers, told who I could and couldn't talk to, and I was put in charge of some pretty demeaning jobs – like washing the outside windows of a storefront and taping down cables.

This was the very production where the producer stood up in front of the entire crew. She announced that this was how she made her living, and that she didn't want to have to work a nine-to-five job. I looked around at all the surrounding production assistants – the ones who weren't getting paid any money. The ones who were working on their one day off from their nine-to-five jobs to make this shitty little film happen. That was the straw that broke the camel's back. At that moment, I decided I simply didn't want to work in film anymore – at least not on anyone else's film. I said goodbye to my fellow interns, and walked off set. It was the only time I ever walked away from a production without at least finishing the day.

◆ ◆ ◆

Looking back, I think there were times where I gave up too easily. Working in film can often times test your passion. How deep are you willing to sink to get what you want? At that moment, I felt I sank deep enough. I wasn't enjoying being on a film set. Most times, I was flat-out miserable. I guess there are times in your life where you realize the thing you've been going after isn't what you thought it would be.

I've heard stories from many other filmmakers about what a pleasure it was to work with such a gifted crew. I hear about situations where everyone got along, and everyone working there wanted to be there. I wish I could have been a part of one of those crews. Because working for smaller productions in Michigan, I never felt like I was meant to be there. In fact, I usually felt that other crew members *judged* me for being there, as if they knew I didn't belong and questioned why I was there.

I was there because like everyone else involved in film production, I liked movies. And the idea of getting to work on movies was really exciting. But when you're dealing with inflated egos – especially egos from *local* talent – it just isn't a fun place to be anymore. Aside from the movies I made, I never really had a positive experience on a film set, aside from the small workshops and competitions. Most of the people I've worked with were either grumpy because they'd been working for twelve hours, or were so full of themselves that they felt they were entitled to treat others like shit.

These are, of course, based on my own experiences. If you work in the film industry – hell, if you're working in a field that is remotely connected to your passion – embrace it, and do everything you can to hold on to it. That's a rare thing. But only do it if you truly believe you were meant to do it. Don't let anyone stop you. Don't listen to those who are jealous, who try to use their own insecurities to bring you down, who think that what you're doing is unobtainable because you're doing something that they don't have the balls to do themselves.

I don't know if I was meant to be a filmmaker. Maybe it's still in the cards. I still have my dreams. My goal is to one day make a film. Just one. I don't need to be the next George Lucas. I don't need a string of successes. I don't even need one. I just want to make one feature-length movie, so that someday, years from now, I can show my kids that it *is* possible.

From the way things have been going, I think I was meant to be a dad. I was meant to be a husband. I'll even go as far to say that I was meant to be a mail carrier. I don't see myself really doing anything else to earn money, and I could be doing a lot worse financially.

But I also see myself as a storyteller. I think in some way, I was always meant for that. I'm not sure what form those stories will take, but the need to tell stories still swells in my heart. Even if they're not committed to celluloid, I can still dream.

Oh, but what it is to dream.

CHAPTER 17:

*The Excitingly Worthless
World of Self-Publishing*

Over the last few years, I've been in a serious debate with myself: books or screenplays?

It's funny. When I first took on this passion for storytelling, I read a lot. Even well into my teens, if I wasn't engaged in a video game or knee-deep in the *Star Wars* trilogy, I had my nose in a book. *Harry Potter, The Dragonlance Chronicles* – those were my caffeine.

It wasn't until my senior year of high school that I became much more focused on movies. And while the dream is still there, and making small, self-contained short films is still in the cards, let's face it: writing is so much easier.

Here's the dilemma: I actually prefer screenwriting to prose. With screenwriting, you follow a rigid format, and it's almost impossible to do without creating some sort of road map. Since one page is the on-screen equivalent to one minute of screen time, a screenplay by definition is pretty short. You also don't get to describe everything in a screenplay, which I enjoy. I've never been very good at laying down atmosphere and playing around with words. Sure, if you beat me with a stick, I could come up with a hundred descriptive adjectives to describe your favorite childhood tree. But I'd much rather just type A tree sways in the wind and be done with it.

If you study film, you'll more than likely hear that a screenplay is a blueprint for your movie, and it is. You're only writing what the audience is going to see and hear. That means there's no room for a character's inner thoughts, and you're definitely not going to be describing what the characters did since birth, unless you're actually crafting a scene in which we're meant to experience it. As a younger writer, it was impossible for me to contain my ideas. I could never stick to a small page count, which irritated most of my Language Arts teachers.

But as I got older, it got harder to find things to write about, much less extensively. Screenwriting was more about my passion for wanting to make movies. It was a much more succinct way to tell a story. The only problem was, no one reads screenplays.

You won't find a "screenplay" section at your local bookstore, and you won't find it on Amazon, either – I've checked. That's because, unless you have a hit movie that has defied expectations and has crept its way into pop culture, no one publishes screenplays. You can easily buy published versions of the scripts for *Star Wars* or *Pulp Fiction* – but those are exceptions to the rule.

Screenplays are typically pitched – and if you're extremely lucky, sold – to Hollywood execs looking to make a movie deal. Which makes success as a screenwriter extremely challenging and daunting. I'm sure you've seen an episode of a sitcom where one character cajoles another character to just up and write a screenplay. That's all well and good if you're an out of work actor staving off boredom – but it's not a surefire way to make a living.

Neither is book writing. In all honesty, both are things you really have to work at to find any amount of success with. But if you ask any writer, you'll probably find that publishing a book is a hundred times more likely, because aside from printing costs, there's not as much of a risk.

For the longest time, the only things I ever had published were a couple of poems I wrote in my creative writing class at Lawrence Tech. They had an on-campus publication called *Prism*, and I remember feeling so excited just to be able to see a couple of things I wrote in print. I knew the likelihood of anyone reading it was slim to none, but I got a kick out of it nonetheless.

One day, out of the blue, I got a radical idea for a screenplay. It wasn't something I intended to produce, but I felt so strongly about the idea that I thought maybe I could send it off to a few contests. It was the quickest turn-around for any project I'd ever written: one month to write a feature-length script.

The story was called *Ushar*. It follows a recently-divorced, award-winning documentary filmmaker who goes off to Africa to document the newly-discovered Ki-amani tribe. When Wallace, our protagonist, finally arrives with all his camera gear, he is shocked to discover that the tribe consists of women and children – but no men. He is also surprised to find that not only are the tribeswomen very welcoming to strangers, but they are awfully flirtatious. Eventually, Wallace ends up in the good graces of one of the locals, a beautiful and fierce tribeswoman named Ki-mun-di. Deciding to be a little spontaneous, Wallace decides to start a relationship with Ki-mun-di, who reciprocates, and the two slowly start to fall for one another. To Wallace's shock, he actually contemplates *marrying* her. Then, at the end of the first act, he discovers what happened to all the men. As part of the wedding ceremony, the men are sacrificed in a tribal ritual called *ushar*. Upon hearing this, Wallace freaks out and, fearing for his life, decides to bail. Ki-mun-di assures Wallace that no harm will come to him, but because of his craven reaction, she can't marry him. Ki-mun-di reveals that the Ki-amani believe heavily in the Afterlife, and the reason the men agree to the ceremony is because their willingness to be sacrificed makes for a strong husband. The Ki-amani women believe that after the ceremony, the spirits of their husbands assist them in the Afterlife. Before the ceremony takes places, the husband ensures that his new bride is pregnant. The unborn child serves as the link between the world of the living and the Afterlife. It is because of Wallace's negative reaction to the concept that Ki-mun-di ultimately falls out of love with him. The second act explores Wallace's ability to come to terms with what *ushar* really is, and because his feelings for Ki-mun-di are so strong, he actually agrees to do the ceremony if she marries him. The second act also introduces Wallace's teenage son, Derek, who comes to visit his dad due to his strained relationship with his mother. Derek has no concept of *ushar* and is left in the dark about it. However, during the third act, Derek accidentally stumbles across the actual ceremony, and at the eleventh-hour Wallace pleads with Derek to save him from ultimately being sacrificed. The final ten pages are an intense chase through the African wilds, as Derek and a severely injured Wallace try to get to safety while the Ki-amani, along with a neighboring tribe, give chase.

I had never written anything like it. The ideas just kept flowing in, like a floodgate. I think part of it came from my own insecurities. I've always been frustrated with my physical appearance. I'm not exactly America's idea of "sexy."

Before you tell me to get over myself, hear me out. I also understand that different cultures have varying ideas about what they consider attractive. In some countries, overweight men are considered extremely sexy. Some cultures prefer women with potbellies. One of my fantasies has always been to be the only man on an island where someone who looks like me is considered attractive by the inhabitants. Then I thought about this irony: with my luck, the only way that would happen is if I had to die. That was where the idea of *ushar* came from. Then, I took that idea even further into the realm of absurdity. What if the protagonist learned about this ritual – and decided to go through with it?

The biggest challenge with that idea was, I knew I'd be asking a lot from my audience. There had to be a reason why the audience bought into this idea of this neurotic man, who fears death above everything else, agreeing to this insane ritual simply because he loves this woman. So, a lot of the story, specifically the second act, deals with the concept of death and how we all cope with it.

I'm also a big fan of the Mel Gibson-directed film, *Apocalypto*. If you haven't seen it, give it a try. It's a little hard to find, but it's really intriguing. It follows a small South American tribe whose village gets invaded by the neighboring Mayans. The idea of the Ki-amani tribe was heavily inspired by this film. It's not an English-language film, but it's riveting from start to finish. The chase in the third act was also heavily inspired by that film.

At the time, I was still in touch with Jody, who would periodically check in and send me information pertaining to screenwriting competitions. Screenwriting competitions are always a gamble because their submission fees are outrageous – they start at $50 a submission – and unless you pay extra, you never know if you're going to get any feedback. But I felt so strongly about the script that I ended up shelling out over a hundred bucks to get direct feedback from the judges.

The feedback I received was surprisingly positive. The writing was sound, the story was engaging and they actually admired the level of world-building. BUT... there was an overall larger problem that kept it from winning any awards, and unfortunately, it wasn't a case of simply adding or deleting a page.

As I explained earlier, I was asking a lot from my audience. The whole concept of Wallace agreeing to this ritual, which ended in certain death, just wasn't believable. It was kind of heartbreaking, because the judge basically said that no studio would greenlight the project because of its concept. But I knew what I was writing, and I was very much aware of how insane it all was. It was a story that I felt strongly about, and that I really wanted to tell.

The other piece of criticism I received was my treatment of the Ki-amani tribe. For this, the only excuse I have is my lack of research. But seriously, when you Google African tribes, you're more than likely going to see some outlandish photos. To the judge's credit, I wrote the Ki-amani tribe as a predominantly primitive group of people who were ignorant to technology, living in a backwards culture even though they were forward-thinking when it came to the idea of death. Essentially, it was a very Hollywood-centric tribe, the kind of thing you might see in an 80's popcorn movie. What a coincidence, since 80's films happen to be my cup of tea.

I wasn't trying to write an 80's film, but I also understood (sort of) where the judge was coming from. I was always curious how an African-American audience would respond to my representation of their culture. Would they be insulted? Would they simply roll their eyes at yet another big-screen betrayal of their homeland? Or would they be engaged enough in the story where it would just be an oversight?

This is a very confusing time. We live in a society where one group of people *acts* offended on behalf of another group of people, even if the group of people in question aren't *that* affected to begin with.

In 2017, Scarlet Johansson starred as Major Kusanagi in the live-action adaptation of the anime, *Ghost in the Shell*. It was a controversial casting choice because Johansson, a Caucasian American actress, was portraying a character whose origin was Japanese – in a film that took place in Japan and stemmed heavily from Japanese roots. Americans were outraged at the "whitewashing", a term that was thrown around a lot even before *Ghost in the Shell* was released.

The reality was, even though American fans were upset,

the choice was immensely popular overseas because Johansson was huge among that demographic. Go figure.

Then again, it was just one person's opinion. I told the story I wanted to tell. Every time I described the story to someone, they flat-out told me it was something they'd pay money to see. Eventually, I'd like to take another stab at it, except this time, maybe I'll try to send it out to some studios. Contests are a great way to get recognition, if you win anything. Who knows? Maybe one day I'll turn it into a novel.

One day, I started researching self-publishing. I researched the topic a decade before, and back then, you had to pay a company a bunch of money up front just to publish a few copies of your manuscript.

Then I stumbled upon this thing on Amazon called Kindle Direct Publishing. It was almost too good to be true. For literally no cost, you could submit something you wrote to Amazon, and Amazon would publish it for free. You set the price, and then Amazon split the cost 70/30. It was essentially targeted for Amazon's e-book format, but then I realized that you could have your work turned into a physical paperback. And it was print-on-demand. This meant that there were no up-front costs. Amazon only printed as many copies as were ordered. There wasn't as much profit with a physical copy, because unlike the e-book format, there were printing costs – but anything I wanted to submit could be transformed into a paperback that I could then display on a bookshelf.

I sifted through my computer files and found several candidates. Among them, there were the original four *Galactic Redemption* stories that I wrote in junior high, not to mention the epic sci-fi novel that I spent all of high school writing long-hand in loose-leaf notebooks, *Battalion Stealth*.

As a testing bed, I submitted the original *Galactic Redemption*. I did some minor editing, mostly dealing with punctuation changes. I didn't want to mess with the story too much.

After all, I was fourteen back when I wrote it – and I wanted my fourteen-year-old self to be preserved in those pages.

Throughout the years, I tried with minimal success to go back and re-edit my older work. No matter what I tried, I ended up making the stories worse as opposed to better – every editor's worst nightmare. I tried making them more serious, more "mature". But I realized that, even though there was an amateurish quality to them, that's what made them fun. To my understanding, Tolkien took the same approach to *The Hobbit*, once he finished *The Lord of the Rings*, and he just wasn't satisfied with how it turned out. That was probably due, in no small part, to the fact that he was at a different point in his life when he wrote that first book. *The Hobbit* is fantastic, and just wouldn't be the same if he tried to match its tone with that of *Lord of the Rings*. In many respects, I think that was one of the problems with the updated *Star Wars* trilogy. In later releases, George Lucas incorporated a lot of elements from his newer, sleeker prequels into the original set of films, and the two styles never really fused together. Again, both trilogies were made at distinctly different times in Lucas's life.

So, I left the majority of the tone of the story intact. I was so excited about seeing it in paperback, that I went to the Post Office the next day and told a couple of my co-workers about it. And one of them went on Amazon that night and placed an order.

Within a week, that same co-worker presented me with the first-ever legitimate paperback copy of *Galactic Redemption*. I had done it. A piece I had created was in print. And someone had spent money on it.

She was quite a sport, asking for my autograph. I indulged her. As pretentious as I felt, I couldn't help feel just *slightly* delighted. Science fiction wasn't her bag, so I knew in a million years she would never actually read it. But the fact that she was supporting my work, even if it was just for a goof, was a thrill.

Within the next month, I submitted all four chapters of the *Galactic Redemption* series for publication. Several co-workers approached me throughout the next few weeks, asking for autographed copies. It put a smile on my face.

None of them were actually going to read them. Most of my co-workers just weren't interested in science fiction. But just the fact that they supported me was enough. I was getting recognition. And the best part for me, honestly, was coming home and seeing actual paperbacks of *my* work on my bookshelf next to the works of Michael Crichton and Stephen King.

In published form, the *Galactic Redemption* books appeared to be more like novellas. The first two books clocked in at sixty pages each, with *Galactic Redemption 4* approaching closer to novel-status.

The next two months were dedicated to editing *Battalion Stealth*. I spent more time with this one, because the story was much larger and there were a lot of things I wanted to fix. Primarily, there was a lot of senseless technobabble that I wanted to streamline or omit altogether. For whatever reason, I used a lot of ellipses, which was common in comic books, but not in prose. I also took out a lot of swearing, only leaving it in when it was necessary. Before high school, I seldom swore in my stories, so I guess I was trying to be more edgy. But as an adult, I realized how distracting it could be if misused.

The biggest change was that, right before publication, I changed the title to *Our Last Nights on Earth*. It was meant to be a play on words, since the central protagonist's name was Retro Knights. The *K* in *Knights* was going to be red, while the rest of the text would be white, signifying that the word had a double-meaning. When I realized how limited I was in creating text for my book cover, I just said "Fuck it" and changed it to *Nights* for simplicity.

In less than six months' time, I had self-published four novellas and a full-length novel. In total, all five pieces netted me a hundred dollars in royalties. You can buy a heck of a lot of coffee with that.

◆ ◆ ◆

Being a self-published writer is bittersweet. It's a hollow victory, because I didn't have to jump through hoops to do it. I knew that in their current states, no self-respecting publisher would publish work from my teenager self. But all I wanted was to see my work in print, and to have a few people enjoy them. And hey, a hundred-dollar profit is nothing to sneeze at, even with a cold.

The point I'm trying to make is, just because you follow your dreams doesn't guarantee success. That comes with a lot of luck, a lot of connections, and an extremely hard work ethic. Not having extra mouths to feed helps, too.

Something I wish I learned a long time ago: whatever you're passionate about, pursue it. Don't try to make a living at it, because it's hard to do, and you'll more than likely let yourself down. Besides, anyone will tell you, if you start making money at your passion, eventually, it just becomes another pain in the ass job.

From a financial standpoint, I have proven time and time again – I am *not* successful at my passion. But I continue doing it because I want to. I need to tell stories, even if no one wants to hear them. That's where the title of this book comes from. A wise Jedi Master once said, "Do, or do not. There is no try." I'm here to say, those who can't do, try anyway. Try your hardest. Whatever your passion is, you owe it to yourself to try it out. After all, I'd rather fail at doing something I love, then having never tried at all.

So, if I may, I'd like to amend that great quote. Try, or try not – who gives a fuck if you fail, as long as you're happy doing it?

EPILOGUE:

My Bullshit Coda

Only now, at the very end, do I realize that what I talked about at the very beginning, my timeless ability to accidentally offend others, really has no bearing on the rest of this book. I'd like to end this by coming around full circle. Hopefully, this will make most of you laugh. Inevitably, it will also offend at least one person. And I'm more than happy to do that, too.

Near the beginning of the COVID-19 pandemic, when everything was being shut down and everyone was being threatened with martial law if they so much as left their houses, the Post Office issued all of its postal workers a piece of paper that stated we were essential workers. That way, if we were ever pulled over, we could present this "essential" piece of paper and avoid a hefty fine.

I thought about the term "essential worker". It was a term that was thrown around a lot during the Holocaust. A Jewish worker had to present a piece of paper showing they were essential to the war effort, and if they failed to do so, they were shipped off to Auschwitz.

It was a scary thought, and a parallel I made immediately. I posted the following message on Facebook: "The Post Office issued me a piece of paper today, declaring that I'm an essential worker. Is it me, or does this sound eerily reminiscent of Auschwitz?" I posted this, of course, with a short clip from the Spielberg film *Schindler's List*, where a one-armed machinist desperately tries to explain that he's an "essential worker" – right before a Nazi shoots him in the fucking head.

Because Facebook is such a warm and forgiving outlet, you can guess how this went down: I was crucified.

Right off the bat, several people commented that the stay-at-home order was nothing like Auschwitz, and that they were offended by my comment. Because people weren't actually being shot, I had no right belittling the Jewish people by making such an embarrassing comparison. Another one of my peers, a Berkley High School alum, now a lawyer, pointed out that it was unconstitutional for local law enforcement to require us to carry around such a piece of paper.

That might be good and well, but I was still issued the paper in the first place.

Then a big political debate ensued. Some were on my side, and were angered because they felt their rights were being taken away by being forced to stay at home. Others continued the argument that there was no comparison, that our governor was an angel from the Heavens above and that we shouldn't mind having a few of our privileges stripped away in order to cooperate with our government.

The biggest jab, though, was when a family member – someone I used to be close with – commented that she couldn't believe how offensive I was, and then went on to say, "But what do I know?" And then another family member – one I almost never get along with – commented back, saying, "You know a lot."

Whenever I post something political, it always starts an unwanted political debate. And I never come out of it feeling good. I feel like shit. I feel like I'm the target for everyone's political defenses. It's just one more reason why I try really hard not to get involved with politics.

Let me clarify – I hate politics, as a rule, but like everyone else, I still take a stand on certain issues. People know me to be a smartass. I used to fight that tooth and nail, until one day I just came to terms with it: I *am* a smartass. That's who I am. That's who I'll always be. I wear that truth like a badge of honor, now. And it's not something I aspire to be. But that's where my sense of humor comes from. It just sucks that my own flesh and blood would just as soon berate me and judge me than accept me for my faults. I accept my cousins for being prudish, stuck-up bitches – so why can't they accept me for this?

Maybe it's because the truth hurts. Is my comparing Auschwitz to a terrifying piece of paper really that alarming? And what strikes me about that incident is, I wasn't even trying to be funny. I wasn't aiming to make any sort of satirical state-ment, that was just how I felt at that point in time. And I think the statement I was making was far more important than all those idiots who feel the need to post what they made for din-ner. Every. Fucking. Night. Of. The. Week.

The problem with all those people who butchered me for making that comparison was that they weren't listening to what I was saying. They didn't want to listen, because the very idea was terrifying to *them*. So, they turned it around, making me feel like the asshole. I ended my part in the conversation by saying, "For god's sake, don't be complacent." Now that I look back, maybe 'complacent' wasn't the right word. But basically, all I was saying was, don't intentionally roll over just because you're told to. Question things. That was something they never taught us in school. Why? Because public school is run by the government. But as we get older, I would hope that most of us question what we're told.

Apparently, most people don't. Most people accept whatever they're told and go along with it. And in the end, I'm the asshole. I'm the one throwing a monkey wrench into the government's master plan.

Don't give me so much credit. I'm a postal worker who occasionally writes a shitty science fiction book. I live in suburbia. Nothing I say matters all that much. But let's not pretend that my ideas are that outrageous. Stop pointing fingers. It's time to take your heads out from your smelly asses and smell the coffee. You can't be offended by everything you hear. Man the fuck up, people. Come to think of it, I like the sound of that. Maybe that'll be the title of my next book.

Man the Fuck Up, by Dr. Lenny Sherman.

Nah. I don't want to offend anyone.